Think Like A Millionaire

A guide to creating a life changing business and finding financial freedom

Josh Grant

JOSH GRANT

THINK LIKE A MILLIONAIRE

Table of Contents

Introduction 7

Part One: Developing a Millionaire Mindset 14

Chapter 1: You Now vs. The Future You 14

Golden Rules for Developing Positive Mindset 16

Develop Your SMART Goals 17

Chapter 2: Visionary 21

Practical Steps to Create Visionary Habit 22

How Visionary Affects the Mindset of a Millionaire 24

Chapter 3: The Growth Mindset 26

Fixed vs. Growth Mindset 26

20 Ways To Develop Growth Mindset 28

Why Growth Mindset Is important In Achieving Goals 34

Chapter 4: The Commitment 37

How To Develop Strong Commitment 38

What To Do If You Want To Stay Committed 40

Top Principles of the Millionaire Mindset 42

Millionaire Trait that You Should Possess 48

Millionaire Signs 50

Part Two: Increasing Your Income 52

Chapter 5: Making Something from Nothing 52

Steps to Wealth Creation... 53

Chapter 6: Starting up A Business. 58

Step-By-Step Guide To Starting A Business 59

Why Starting Up a Business Can Make You a Millionaire 61

Things To Do Before Starting a Business... 63

Mistakes To Avoid When Starting a Business..................................... 66

Chapter 7: Building Passive Income Streams 70

Active Income vs. Passive Income – Which One Is Suitable? 70

How to Shift Your Livelihood to Passive Income 72

Stages to Solid Passive Incomes Today 73

Smart Passive Income Ideas Millionaires' Need 75

Chapter 8: Adding a Side Hustle to your 9-5 Job 77

How to Develop Side Hustles 77

How to Effectively Build a Side Hustle 78

Part Three: Saving & Investing... 81

Chapter 9: Emergency Fund 81

What Is An Emergency Fund? 82

Reasons You Need an Emergency Fund.. 82

Steps to Help You Grow Your Emergency Fund Faster	85
Where Do I Put My Emergency Fund?	86
How Much Should I Save?	87
Overcoming Obstacles When Saving for an Emergency Fund	88
Chapter 10: Think of Retirement	89
Finding Out How Much You Will Need	90
Finding Ways to Set Money Aside Now	90
Analyzing Tax-Deferred Ways to Save	92
Allow Your Employer to Help You	94
Invest In Yourself	96
Chapter 11: Investing in Stock Market	97
Day Trading	98
Benefits and risks in day trading	99
Swing Trading	100
The good side of swing trading	101
The Right Market	102
Long Term Investing	102
Principles of Diversity	103
Be patient with your plan.	104
Setting Short-Term and Long-Term Goals	104

Taking Profit 106

Chapter 12: Real Estate Investment 108

Types of Real Estate Investments 108

Getting Acquainted with Real Estate Investment 110

Seeking Cash Buyers for Real Estate 114

Finding Motivated Sellers 115

Finding Lenders to Fund Your Deals 117

Sealing Your First Deal 117

Chapter 13: Investing in Cryptocurrency 118

What are Cryptocurrencies? 118

Getting Ahead 119

Choosing an Exchange platform 120

How many cryptos Should You Buy? 121

Top Coins to Invest In 122

Chapter 14: Investing Tips From the World's Successful Investors 127

Motivation Hub: Inspiring Stories of Successful People 134

Conclusion 153

Resources 156

Introduction

Whatever may be said in praise of destitution, investment, and unemployment, the fact remains that it's not possible to live a successful life without planning. Let me put this straight; it is impossible to suddenly become wealthy without making any plans for it. Well... unless a wealthy relative leaves you trust funds.

Every person naturally wants to become rich. Maybe rich is a strong word here. I will put it this way: every person naturally wants comfort and security. However, we must first understand the realms of success in life. Not just to understand success but to become committed to it.

It is not just about making money. You can make money from nothing - something we will see in this book. So, it is beyond finding ways to make money. It is about your orientation. Your thought process, commitment, and planning are instrumental in this journey. How far are you willing to go? When there are obstacles on the way, what do you do? Therefore, it is crucial to FIRST think like a millionaire.

In a nutshell, before you can become a millionaire, you must, first, think like a millionaire.

This book will arm you with the tools you need to persevere and succeed. It is important to know that on this journey to attain wealth, your zeal, desire, and hunger for success will prove to be very instrumental. See, there is nothing wrong with wanting to be a millionaire, but sometimes people fail to face the challenges that come their way. In today's world, you need to learn to be proactive if you want to be rich. If possible, select the right partner and keep yourselves motivated. This will lessen you towards achieving your set goals.

Now get this, having millions in your bank account or investment portfolios worth millions is the goal of every person imbibing that millionaire mindset. However, there is just so much that you can achieve by having that mindset. For instance, the growth mindset is a huge part of millionaires. With this, you are exposed to so many concepts that might not make you richer but add substance to you.

What do I mean by this?

Sooner or later, you will get tired of your 9-5 job. (When this happens, how will you cope with your commitment that requires enough money to stand well?) Your 9-5 might not be secure or doesn't cover all the bills. Most importantly, millionaires are not made from 9-5 jobs.

There is where the millionaire mindset kicks in. That mindset will help you figure out your next step. For instance, investing, saving, and creating multiple passive income streams is one way to build wealth worth millions.

In the 2021 stock market in the United States, Statista disclosed that, out of the world population, about 56% invest in the stock market and plan of their retirement. Anything above 50% might seem great; however, we still have the opportunity to up that number. This opportunity starts inside that brain of yours. You need that mindset that assures commitment to achieve a sustainable lifestyle. A man or woman develops their mind by making use of opportunities. The object of life is development, so how do you manage your time to achieve these goals? Meanwhile, everything that lives, has an inalienable right to all the growth we can attain. Therefore, this is the right time to think and explore different solutions to become a millionaire. Build your mental, spiritual, and physical development to maintain a suitable life.

Since you have known your mission, becoming a millionaire will be attainable if you set a daily target. I am sure you've seen the success stories of people like Warren Buffet on TVs? But do you think those people inherited their money? Of course, NO! as

becoming a millionaire has nothing to do with your family wealth. Besides, it has everything to do with you and how you work to make the dream come to reality.

According to Forbes, Millions of the world's populations are now working in jobs that didn't exist ten years ago. With this in mind, training and lifelong learning about investments are the keys to rapid changes in today's economy and how we can create something out of nothing.

Yes, let me say that again: create wealth out of nothing. You will be hearing more of this and just exactly how it is possible.

Not having capital can result in setbacks, but you can create that capital. With the capital, you will expand through avenues like investing. Starting a business with limited capital requires you to diversify. Traditionally, we can begin the process of looking for business opportunities and check the ones that meet our little money. Next, we establish a goal and fill the gap with the capital. With this, you'll see that you've created a business by creating capital from your little start-up.

Investment today has evolved from scratch, different from the conventional approach of the 1950s (Investopedia). Now, investors have since recognized the importance of sustainable investment. Yet, the complexity of time forces today still yields different opinions from humans. This means time and investment contribute to what could make you become a successful being. How do you manage your time with investment? Answering this question will help you to develop the right mindset to become a millionaire in the future. In this life-changing investment book, I'll show you how system-level investors affect the stability of finance and environmental systems in today's digital world.

Similarly, this book is for new and existing investors who believe in transition. There may be companies or individual investors who would want to achieve a lifetime goal. Whoever they may be, I will definitely show them what, why, and how thinking like a millionaire can make them achieve their goals in this book. Not only that, but how to integrate this new way of thinking like a millionaire into their current practice.

The extent to which the modern economy depends on investment and digital currencies was revealed by business leaders a few years ago. According to the claim, the growth statistic has surpassed more than 60 percent of physical investment. *(Investopedia)*. Despite all the dramatic increase in the number of companies, there is more technological advancement today. Global financial markets have evolved substantially due to the pace of technical, regulatory changes over the past years. Aside from that, technology has made regular activities such as banking more efficient. Similarly, trading in the financial market has dramatically improved in recent times.

Nonetheless, trading and investing are still often regarded as the best way to grow rich.

To put it into a nutshell, investments are evolving, and the best way to take advantage of this golden opportunity is to utilize that millionaire mindset of yours and invest. I mean, you can't depend on those 9-5 jobs forever, especially if you are looking to become a millionaire. The means to making money has transcended; that's why there are tons of ways to become wealthy today. No need to visit the stock exchanges to buy a share of a company. You can do that online from the comfort of your home. What about print on demand business? Print-on-demand services are a lucrative business that offers an alternative way to bypass time and investment. Also, it reduces the risk associated with managing inventory and letting you go from creating to selling custom products. However, this book will teach you the best possible ways to accomplish that. You will learn

- Developing a positive mindset to become rich

- How to increase your income and make something from nothing

- What to know before and after your retirement lifestyle

- Saving and different investment tips in today's world

- What to learn from various inspiring stories of successful investors

- How to add a side hustle to your 9-5 job

- Top principles of the millionaire mindset

- How to be successful while starting up a new business

- How to achieve long-time investment goals

You see, on this journey, you won't only learn how to develop the mindset to make millions but how to make the millions. I mean, it will be useless having a mindset and not knowing what to do with it, right? That's not the plan. Here's what I have for you: first, think like a millionaire, and then work as a millionaire. You *will* become a millionaire. It is that straightforward.

So, why don't we get started?

Part One: Developing a Millionaire Mindset

Chapter 1: You Now vs. The Future You

The secret of health and a positive mindset is not to mourn for the past but instead think about the future. You can live in the moment wisely and begin to think about your future. Eliminating nonessential possessions today has contributed to what grieved our emotions, and this usually keeps us stuck. Therefore, you should clarify your personality, mindset, development in the present moment and future. In a nutshell, eliminating anything that won't contribute to your success is essential. That's why you need to focus on what you're doing now and use your previous experience as a source of motivation to achieve your goal.

From Forbes, we discovered that one of the best, unforeseen consequences of simplifying our lives is to live in the present moment. While doing this, it's highly crucial to think about the future. How do you feel about the future while enjoying the present moment? Now, let me use this example as an illustration. Imagine you buy two eggs to eat, and you think of eating them in the morning. I am sure you'll be thinking of what to eat for afterward, right? Did you get the explanation and what it entails?

Notwithstanding, the eggs illustrated what you are doing in the present moment while what you're about to eat in the long run constitutes your plans and goals. Subsequently, this is what happens when you are trying to develop a millionaire mindset. What are your plans now, and what could be the future for you? Perhaps, living in the past could rob your mind and restrict you from today's enjoyment. So, the only important thing is to describe your potential now to identify what you are capable of achieving in the near future.

With that goal in mind, start your day with a smile and always think that each day is full of endless possibilities. You are in control of your mindset; you can achieve whatever you set your mind to. With this, keep it optimistic, expectant, be intentional, and find yourself in the right state of mind. More so, forgive past hurts, love what you do, dream about the future, think like a millionaire and work hard today. If you have any hindrance, stop worrying and believe instead beyond the old solution to problems.

While you're progressing, many things could bring you down. The first thing to get rid of is addiction. Always know that addiction in your life will definitely hold you hostage. In fact, addiction will keep you from living a completely free life and remove your focus to achieving greatness in life. If you choose to evaluate your life now, would you rate up to 50 percent? Are you an addicted person? Now, evaluate whether you meet up to the addiction level. As it stands now, if you are above 50 percent, you have a certain level of addiction in which you'll need to get rid of. Therefore, you need to abstain from anything that could affect your future. Be ambitious and believe in yourself to achieve the goals.

➢ Golden Rules for Developing Positive Mindset

To take advantage of 21st-century digitalization, you must be innovative. As a person wanting to be rich in a few years to come, remember you will need to plan ahead, right? Interesting! So, are you clear about your future goals? Meanwhile, be aware that goal settings provide you a benchmark for determining whether you are actually on the right track to success. Think about it and digest the fact.

Also, do you know that having a million dollars in the bank is only proof of success if you are able to multiply it and make it multi-millions? So, if your goal is to be rich in the nearest future, you will need to develop a positive mindset and know the golden rules that'd keep you active to achieve greatness. Here are the golden rules of goal settings and a positive mindset. Read carefully to understand what it entails.

Set Goals That'll Inspire You

The first step to developing the millionaire mindset is to set the goals that will motivate you. Moreover, make sure you set the goals that'd interest you in the long run. If possible, set goals that relate to the high priorities in your life. Now you will be able to achieve a desirable outcome. Motivation is the key to start a millionaire mindset. So, to maximize the likelihood of success, you need to feel a sense of urgency in your attitude.

➢ Develop Your SMART Goals

I am sure you might have heard of the acronym SMART. If not, the simple fact it helps your goals to be powerful. Besides, it was developed by George Doran, Arthur Miller, and James Cunningham in their 1981 article. Naturally, there are many variations to what SMART stands for, but the essence and the validity of the acronym include the following.

S= Specific

M= Measurable

A= Attainable

R= Relevant/Realistic

T= Time-Bound

Setting Unique/Specific Goals: Before you start thinking like a millionaire, you must define your goal. This is what would lead you to believe in several ways to become rich. While setting your goals, make it easy to be able to achieve your future. You can think of different investment options on how to make a considerable income afterward.

Is Your Goal Measurable? Before you can think like a millionaire, including price, dates, and how you'll be able to measure your goals, don't just think like a millionaire but measure your million worth in the long run. If your goal is simple, you should think of the challenges and how to overcome them as times go by.

Set Attainable Goals for Yourself: While you are thinking like a millionaire, be realistic with your goals and future achievements. How do you intend to make your millions? What are the requirements, and what kind of job do you want to engage in that would make you succeed as a millionaire? You will only demoralize yourself and erode your confidence when you are unable to make millions after thinking like a millionaire for years. That is why it's crucial to set attainable goals.

Develop Relevant/Realistic Goals: Your millionaire mindset must have a deadline. Again, this means that you will be able to know the right time to celebrate your achievement. By keeping your goals aligned with this, you will develop the focus you need to become a millionaire. This means that if you set widely scattered and inconsistent goals, you may squander your time and life away.

Set Time-Bound Goals: As mentioned earlier, a realistic time bond is essential while planning your goals. Don't just be thinking like a millionaire. Instead, set a time frame and how you'll be able to achieve these goals. For example, you can decide to invest in real estate, cryptocurrency, or other things that'll increase your earnings in the future.

Write Out Practical Steps: These steps are often missed in the process of setting a reasonable goal. You get to focus on the outcome after making your plans. This is especially important if your goals are big. Whether it's a long-term goal or a short-term goal, action plans and practical steps are vital to achieving your goals. Below are the practical steps to developing the right mindset.

Start by brainstorming all the tasks you need to complete before achieving your goals

Analyze and look at current status to know whether you can achieve the goals

Double-check your analysis with SCPEMES; meaning Space, Cash, People, Equipment, Materials, Expertise, and Systems

Learn and revise your plan

Manage bigger projects and set deadlines for yourself

Write your goal in the present to meet future goals

Give your goal the control test it deserves

List out the benefits of thinking like a millionaire and the obstacles within

Highlight the objectives that'd let you track your progress efficiently

Create a plan of action and share your goals

Stick with Your Goals: Goal setting is much more than simply saying you want to achieve greatness. Rather, you clearly define the exact millionaire you want to become. Your end destination may remain quite similar in the long run if you don't plan well. So, it's better to stick with your goals and believe in what you can do. Besides, make sure the value, necessity, purpose, and relevance of your goal remain high.

Chapter 2: Visionary

Getting rich and achieving financial freedom has been a dream for many, but we fail to make a practical step to achieve these goals. If you don't know the right formula to study, the first thing to know is the visionary. According to Oxford Advanced English Dictionary Wikipedia, a visionary is a person that can envision the future. The visionary state is quite easy to follow as it involves meditation, lucid dreams, daydreams, or arts.

Now, the ability to get a clearer picture of the future is to create visionary habits. In fact, management experts use visualization (Forbes) to implement new ideas and predict the future. Some even conceive it as the ability to form a picture of what they want and how they would make it happen. For these reasons, being a visionary will help you develop the mindset of a millionaire. This is demonstrated by a growing body of literates that goals can be obtained from courses in visionary thinking.

Becoming a visionary may also function as a secular prophet. It allows you to communicate with the mind and figure out why, what, and how you'll be able to achieve your goals in the long run. In that sense, a visionary may allow you to see what something could be long before it actually happens. A practical example is the story of STEVE JOBS, who was an American business magnate, industrial designer, and media proprietor. He is often called a visionary because he was ahead of his time, implementing new ideas that are pioneering in the technology field, so you can imbibe his trait.

While imbibing visionary traits, be sure that you're innovative enough to know what the future holds. By extension, you'll need to be specific about your goals. How do you want to become a millionaire? Do you want to invest or sit down and keep thinking without taking steps? I'm sure you'll love to make progress. That way, follow Ted Nelson's (an investor) explanations as he referred to visionary as a connection with the Internet. This means that as you envision the future, you will need to evolve with it just like the Internet, as it is used as a tool to understand innovation and everything happening around the world. Provide a glimpse into the future by making use of the Internet.

➢ Practical Steps to Create Visionary Habit

Since being a visionary can lead you through your future goals, it's high time to know the practical steps. While it may be true that some persons are born to anticipate the future, there are other options if you lack such natural talents. Here, we have compiled the practical steps to create visionary habits today.

Integrate Disparate Ideas to Be Productive

Innovation is a term that encompasses the reapplication of existing technology. So, the act of connecting disparate thoughts and theories together to produce new thoughts represents visionary habit. So, if you want to achieve that millionaire mindset, you'll need to integrate disparate ideas to be productive.

See the Business from Outside-In Perspective

When you're developing the millionaire mindset, seeing the business or any investment from an outside point of view is enlightening. Besides, this practice can inform new ways of thinking that a better approach to identifying your potentials. Therefore, see the millionaire from an outside-in perspective. However, think about how you'll become if you're to be a millionaire in your present moment. This will guide you to the future.

Think, Win, and Understand Reciprocity

Being a visionary leader means you'll have to think, win and understand reciprocity. This will help you realize that a successful outcome requires cooperation and not an intense competition with anyone. Also, become a problem-solver and focus on resolution, not justification. Besides, take steps to prevent minor deviations from becoming a significant block to achieve your goals.

Surround Yourself with Inspiration

Successful investors like Steve Jobs and Bill Gates may have started their businesses out of their garages, but they surround themselves with inspiration. This will fast-track the ticket to a better and high version of yourself. Whether you're thinking for the long-term or short-term, this will help you design a life you love.

Align Your Habits with Your Vision

This also constitutes another practical step to create visionary habits. Exercise your mind every day, commit yourself to think like you've achieved the goals already. This will reflect the version you're trying to possess in the future. Also, identify the specific goals that connect to your overall vision and set a target for each. Meanwhile, don't underprice yourself, as this can make you stand out and make your dream come true.

➢ How Visionary Affects the Mindset of a Millionaire

We all start life free of a mindset. In the long run, our exposure to different behaviors settles into being our attitude, and simultaneously our attitude coalesces into being our mindset. Just like the son of a billionaire won't get worried about investing part of his money, the son of a shopkeeper will definitely worry. What do you think is the problem? Not to worry, each individual mindset is different from one another. You can't expect the son of a billionaire to think the same way as the son of a shopkeeper. This simple illustration constitutes how vision affects the mindset of every individual.

Now, how does vision affect the mindset of a millionaire? Remember that mindset itself is a neutral expression. Your thoughts and plans determine whether it's going to be a positive mindset or the negative one. For instance, the son of the billionaire, as illustrated earlier, may not value money. With this, the mindset of a billionaire has become an obstacle to his profit, while the shopkeeper's son may think big enough to maximize profits in the future.

In mystical terms, focusing on strategies and meditating on your future goals could make you strive hard. So, you'll need to use the mindset while seeking solutions and possibilities. When you meditate and see the vision of what you'd love to become in the near future, you react to the attitude and change your perspective about life. This will help you find hidden trends to achieve your goals and objectives.

Furthermore, by being a visionary, there are certain traits you need to possess. The journey to think as a millionaire depends on specific characteristics and how you react to your mindset. Do you think you can achieve the goal? If YES, you CAN, and if NO, you CAN'T; that's how being a visionary describes you. Some of the traits that visionaries share are they work hard, make more money, do not persist without analysis, and build great teams and connections.

Chapter 3: The Growth Mindset

The growth mindset is another trait of developing the millionaire mindset. Aside from that, it is a tendency to believe that you can grow. This assumes our intelligence, character, and creative ability in a meaningful way. However, this growth mindset is based on the belief that your fundamental qualities can cultivate through your efforts. With this mindset, you can develop a positive attitude and achieve greatness.

On the flip side, a growth mindset is what we desire for long-term success and achievement. Do you believe that you were born and raised with a fixed set of intelligence and abilities? Or do you think that your ideas are ever evolving? If you said yes, you have what is referred to as a growth mindset.

Don't worry if you currently have a fixed mindset – you can develop a growth mindset with time. However, developing a positive attitude could contribute to a more meaningful life because the range of experience will be considerably broader. To understand more about growth mindset, there's a need to know how to develop the growth mindset, what it takes to be successful, and many others.

➢ Fixed vs. Growth Mindset

Before I explain the process and how to develop the growth mindset, you'll need to understand the differences between the growth mindset and the fixed mindset. For a clear explanation, the concept will be explained according to the point listed below. Without further ado, take a look at the differences.

Growth Mentality: An individual with a fixed mindset always thinks that people are born to be unique, and they also have different talents to become successful. A person with a growth mindset always believes in his/her potential. They work hard to achieve their goals and always overcome any challenges that come their way.

Fear of Failure: A person with a fixed mindset can quit when challenges come their way, thereby affecting their millionaire goals. On the flip side, a growth mindset individual will always learn from challenges as it's part of achieving their goals. Besides, if one is not careful, fear of failure can weigh you down, so you need to employ the right tricks or tools to change your mindset towards achieving your millionaire goals.

Consistency and Flexibility: A fixed mindset person dwells in their past behavior, thinking that achieving goals requires practice and specific skills. Meanwhile, someone with a growth mindset asks themselves questions about frequent failures. Instead of criticizing themselves, they rather work hard, remain consistent with becoming a millionaire, and develop a flexible approach to be successful. So, it's better to promote a growth mindset by praising your intelligence and establish vulnerability as a powerful tool that would make you realize your potential.

➤ 20 Ways to Develop Growth Mindset

There are many ways to develop a growth mindset in today's digital world. While it may seem challenging, we have compiled the best ways to build the growth mindset on thinking like a millionaire. Moreover, this will change your mindset from a fixed to a growth mindset that may be daunting. Without further ado, below are the twenty ways to develop a growth mindset.

- Consider Your Challenges as an Opportunity

As a person who wants to develop the right mindset to become a millionaire, you'll need to face your challenges bravely. If you find yourself terrified in the face of a severe challenge, stop, and reframe the situation. Each challenge is an opportunity that invites you into a new experience that is a sort of adventure.

- Pay Attention to Your Thought

If you've not included this in your plan, it's high time you start the process. Start to pay attention to your words and your mind. If your words are low or dark, the result may come as you think. So, it's advisable to watch yourself and how you feel in certain situations. Besides, replace negative thoughts with more positive ones to build your mindset and replace it with a long-term goal mindset.

- Avoid Seeking Approval from Others

If you want to develop a growth mindset, you should get rid of seeking approval from others. Moreover, you can cultivate self-acceptance and self-approval. This will allow you to understand your capabilities and what you're likely to achieve in the long run. Remember that you are the only person that wants to achieve the millionaire goal, so impress yourself with what you have and avoid seeking other people's approval in any situation.

- Have a Sense of Purpose

  Having a sense of purpose is one of the factors that contribute to having the right mindset. Have you ever asked yourself if life feels like it is purpose-driven? If yes, define yourself what purpose do you want to achieve in life. Thinking like a millionaire can only make you start the process of being successful but building the millions contribute to the target you've developed.

- Take a New Step to Authenticity

  Pretending to be someone else can lead you astray. In fact, it makes you a fake person and also diminishes what you have to offer to yourself and to the world. Becoming truly authentic is a process that takes time and lots of inner work. But once you're able to achieve this, you'll achieve your goals. Not only that, but it will put you in the growth mindset to become the millionaire you crave for.

- Stay Away from Criticism

  It's advisable that you always turn your criticism around until you find it as a gift. Someone else can see what you're doing from another point of view. They may have valuable suggestions and can easily develop a growth mindset. You can embrace the same method for personal growth.

- Learn from Past Experience

Learning from experience and previous mistakes is no doubt the key to be greater. If you can learn from your experience or mistakes, then you can make fewer mistakes in the long run. This can sometimes calm the fear of trying something new and lead you to achieve a positive growth mindset.

- Be Realistic with Your Goals

Always understand that the key to achieving a long-term goal is perseverance. While planning to become a millionaire, be realistic with your vision. Don't make plans that you can't achieve. It takes time to learn a new skill and how to become a good lawyer, so you should understand that to grow your mindset requires hard work, time, and patience.

- Avoid speeding While Growing.

Speed is not important in the process of growing your mindset. This is because the result is less focused. Instead, try and engage yourself or put effort into the process, no matter how long it takes to achieve your goals. Remember, focusing on the process often improves results and yields a positive result in the long run.

- Cultivate Resilience along the Way

While you're developing a growth mindset, always own your attitude. If you've set your goals and you're planning to achieve them sooner or later, make an effort to develop the right mindset. Always persist that opportunities will come, so cultivate resilience along the way. This is because you are remodeling your mind, and that's a pretty wonderful thing to look after.

- Practice Mindfulness and Appreciate the Journey

Mental and physical activities are another way to develop a growth mindset. Appreciate the journey and surround yourself with people that will push you towards achieving the goals. When you are fixated on the outcomes, you miss out on valuable things. This can even hinder you from achieving growth. Remember, a growth mindset always sees beauty in struggling because he/she will get a desirable result.

- Place Your Effort before Talent

If you want to build the growth mindset, part of the things to put into consideration is to place your effort before talent. Hard work should always be rewarded before inherent skill, that's why many people achieve their goal in today's world. If possible, you can highlight the relationship between growth and learning. With this, you'll be able to identify what you need in the long run.

- Be Optimistic About the Future

If you're willing to think like a millionaire, the first step to growth is to be optimistic about the future. Always remember that an optimistic person is someone that finds opportunity in anything he/she is willing to achieve. That way, you can be more successful and achieve your goal than the pessimistic people. Aside from that, optimistic people find comfort and stretch their limits to the maximum level.

- Understand the 'Why" of the Business

According to bestselling author Simon Sinek, people hardly buy what you do but instead why you do it. That way, you can start thinking about whether your goals match your passion. Also, you can try and experience something new. Recall an incident in your life, and this could help you achieve your goal in the long run. Once you're able to discover this, you can grow your business and make your mark in the world.

- Always Be Accountable for Your Actions

Despite all the challenges that come your way, there are possibilities that you can still achieve your goal. Besides, when you're faced with challenges, be the first to acknowledge them and hold yourself accountable. It may be tough and painful, but you can achieve attainable goals through correction while improving yourself at the same time.

- Bring Positivity to Yourself

THINK LIKE A MILLIONAIRE

One of the best ways to bring positivity to yourself is by celebrating others. When you celebrate others, you can be motivated to achieve your set goals and objectives. This is why you see successful investors celebrating their colleagues. In other words, people with a positive growth mindset do understand that celebrating others on their achievement doesn't mean they are failing, or they should start questioning their own success story.

- Take Time to Evaluate Yourself

    If something is going wrong or possibly not as planned, don't force the process. Instead, take a step back and understand your weakness. By doing this, you'll see missteps, and you'll definitely need to adjust and avoid them not to result in another unforeseen occurrence in the future. As you progress while thinking like a millionaire, take time to evaluate yourself. With this, you'll be able to achieve a desirable result.

- Develop Active Listening Skills

    Listening skills contribute to how you think. If we have poor listening skills, achieving the millionaire goal may be quite daunting. In fact, it may even result in a fixed mindset. To avoid such problems, you'll need to develop active listening skills. Oftentimes, when you're unable to listen, you'll have a mental block that may interfere with your growth mindset.

- Get Out of Your Comfort Zone Intentionally

Sometimes, getting out of your comfort zone allows you to achieve greatness in life. In order to grow, think about how the growth will affect your lifestyle in the long run. Imagine being able to smoothly gravitate towards opportunities for innovation when you're out of your comfort zone. With this, you can build the right mindset and take a big step to achieve something creative and result oriented.

- Limit Protecting your Ego.

Don't let protecting your ego get between you to the extent that it changes your attitude. This is because; having ego protection can limit your happiness and restrict you from achieving the millionaire goal. So, prepare to challenge your ego as this may limit your beliefs and assumed limitations. Additionally, try and improve your emotional intelligence to open different paths to success in every area of your life.

➢ Why Growth Mindset Is Important in Achieving Goals

Have you ever thought about the impact of this growth mindset to achieve a desirable goal? Well, the simple, most important factor in achieving success is through the growth mindset. Whether you crave to achieve a personal goal or a professional goal that builds certain skills, a growth mindset is one of the fundamental ingredients to be successful. Below are the key reasons why a growth mindset impacts success.

— It Helps to Formulate a Winning Perspective

One of the first things to know about this growth mindset is that it helps to formulate a winning perspective. Moreover, when it comes to success, formulating a winning perspective is essential. Besides, the only thing that can make this possible is the growth mindset. Also, the truth remains that the growth mindset has to do with an individual perspective. This means whatever you digest on your mind is what you'll be able to achieve in the long run. So, formulating the right mindset will make you become a winner.

— It Helps to Develop Healthy Self-esteem

Talking about a growth mindset without self-esteem and confidence is incomplete. That's why we recommend you to know why you're willing to think like a millionaire before you start the process. To successfully accomplish any worthwhile feat, you must be capable of achieving the set goals in the long run. Mindset is a strong possible one to develop healthy self-esteem, and it is also an important tool that affects our daily lives. So, become the gatekeeper of your mind and plant the seed for inspiration.

— It Helps to Improve Your Degree of Adversity

No matter what goal you seek, the path of your success includes the degree of adversity. This is where mindset plays a crucial role in achieving greatness. In fact, after facing extreme hardship, feel free to be justified in succumbing to defeat. This is a true statement that'll help you to retain the power of a resilient mindset.

— It Helps You Set Underlying Goals

Goal setting is a multi-facet process that requires a positive mindset. Nevertheless, without the proper mindset taking a step further might be difficult. So, with the help of a growth mindset, you'll be able to set underlying goals and dig deep to succeed. If you're ready to command your result, it's better to develop the right growth mindset now.

— It Drives the Mindset to Direct Focus

Mindset is a critical driver to success. Therefore attaining your results constitute a positive mindset. Since a growth mindset will help you focus more, you don't have to waste time complaining about circumstances. Instead, create the mindset that drives focus and helps you to achieve your long-term goals.

Chapter 4: The Commitment

This is the best phase of life that contributes to becoming a millionaire. In any sphere of life, commitment is essential to be able to get a positive result in the long run. Whether they are personal career goals or the goal of an organization, commitment is one of the keys to success. You must always accept that not all things will go as you planned. When you experience any challenge during the process, don't get frustrated. Instead, stay committed and create a path to achieving your goals.

However, you may not be in full control of the event you're dealing with, but when you stick to it, you will eventually get what you have been craving. Most people falsely think they can be successful or committed to their goals in a few days, but when obstacles arise, they quickly lose motivation. With this, they can keep procrastinating on their goal until it disappears. If you want to develop the millionaire mindset, you'll have to make commitment your priority.

Furthermore, always understand that the desire to do whatever it takes to achieve a goal is different from commitment. You may have the desire at first, but when you're not committed, you may lose the urge to be successful. Now, let's talk about how you can develop a commitment to your goals.

➢ How To Develop Strong Commitment?

Always remember that commitment is not something that falls from the sky; you develop the mindset and work towards it. To be committed, you'll need to identify your why. Now, ask yourself this question; *why did you think acting now may lead you to the right path of your goal?*

Essentially, your 'why' can be seen as the key factor to maintain strong commitment. Since it's all the way your life will improve, it's crucial to stay committed. Identify your "why," and this will allow you to scale through when challenges come your way. This is because your why is what keeps you going and thinking that you'll never give up on achieving your set goals and objectives. Below are the ways to develop strong commitment in today's digital world.

Find it Easy to Create Successful Habit.

Whether you want to achieve something great or you're planning to develop the right mindset, it's vital to create a successful habit. If possible, keep your eye open, concentrate and ensure that you know exactly what you want. Besides, always keep in mind that no one can hit your target except you.

- Focus on Your Goal-Not Fear

If you want to develop a strong commitment, you'll need to focus more on your goals and not the fear of losing in the long run.

Irrespective of how disciplined you are, focusing on your goal allows you to be successful.

- Always Focus on Smaller Victories

    If you want to stay committed to your goals, always focus on smaller victories. Just like Bruce Lee said, a goal is not always meant to be reached; it often serves simply as something to aim at (Kirsten NOACK). With this in mind, you'll be able to achieve your goal. For example, if your goal is to run a marathon (42km), you might think for a while to realize the goal. It might be a two-month project and completing your plans will allow you to have a good sense of sense-confidence.

- Discover Why You're Pursuing the Goal

    Undoubtedly, this remains the most challenging part of becoming successful in today's world. While you're setting plans to be successful, discover why you're pursuing the goal. If possible, discover an insatiable hunger. Have you ever asked that; what are the things that make some people pursue their goal with a vehement desire, unlike others? This has been my interest for many years, and the answer is that; successful people are unrelenting towards pursuing their goal. So, if you want to develop a strong commitment, try, and discover why you're pursuing the goal.

- Never Give Up and Never Give In

Quitting is a lesson, and that's one of the reasons to stay committed. Don't quit before you achieve your goal. Instead, invest in yourself, and take drastic measures to save the goal. If you quit somewhere along the line, achieving your goal may be difficult. Do you know why people give up on their goals? Now, check these major reasons why people quit on their goals.

Lack of faith and vision

Perfectionism and not being able to overcome challenges.

Inability to keep commitments due to several failure histories.

These three factors work together. All you need to know is that the more you fail, the less your commitment becomes. So, to overcome the challenges and focus more on your goal, you'll have to keep your head up and never give up when there are challenges. Fight perfectionism, have faith, believe in yourself, and fight failure history to stop it from repeating itself.

➤ What to Do If You Want To Stay Committed

There are many things to do if you want to stay committed to your goal. Remember that if you want to become a millionaire, you'll have to stay committed to it. Procrastination may stop you from achieving it when you don't have a strong and growth-oriented mindset. However, you can stick with your goal through the good and bad times. We have compiled sustainable ways on what to do to stay committed. Below, we have compiled sustainable ways.

THINK LIKE A MILLIONAIRE

Set Realistic Goals – We will continue to emphasize setting a realistic goal. To stay committed to becoming a millionaire, know whether you're capable of achieving your set goals. In fact, you can put it this way; if you become a millionaire today, how would you feel? It's far better to think about what those millions would contribute to your life than to set goals alone.

Revisit/Revise Your Goal Frequently – If you want to become a millionaire, you can only achieve it when you revisit your goal frequently. Know that setting a goal isn't a one-and-done deal. It requires a proper check and something that you'll make a regular habit. To check your progress, you can ask yourself whether what you're doing is right or wrong. Through this, you can evaluate the setbacks and adjust your modes of working accordingly.

Set Routines to Make Millions – Since you already develop the millionaire mindset, it's essential to set the routines to make these millions. Although it might seem boring at first, they can take you to places you never imagined. By and large, millionaires didn't get to where they are through procrastination or by winging it. Rather, they take time to cultivate good habits and set routines to make their millions.

Motivate Yourself – Sometimes, what you planned may not work as you want. In this situation, stay inspired by motivating yourself. One great way to do that is to look at successful millionaires in business. Think about their challenges and how they overcome them. With this, you'll be able to get rid of the negative mindset that comes during the process of achieving your goal.

Give Yourself a Pep Talk – Giving yourself a pep talk is one of the best ways to stay committed to your goals. If possible, keep a visual in front of you, identify your purpose, and set daily weekly, or monthly reminders to achieve these goals. Aside from that, you can also map out concrete goals, pinpoint your habits, and visualize your vision or achievements in the coming years.

Manage Your Time – Keep in mind that staying committed requires you to manage your time effectively. Set up a good system that would allow you to manage your time and stick to your goals. If the ones you set don't work, spend your time wisely and avoid wasting your time at all costs.

➤ Top Principles of the Millionaire Mindset

Getting rich is the dream of many but achieving this goal may require a daunting process. What successful millionaires do of "use) is by following the principles of the millionaire mindset. While applying this method, you don't need to fear. Instead, turn around and follow the path to financial freedom.

For most people, having a million dollars remains a dream and nothing more. Why do you think that happened? Well, it's because most people don't set their minds to achieve their goals. By following these simple principles, you'll be able to develop the right mindset. Over time, you'll also learn how to think like a rich man or woman. These principles are divided into series, and we'll be taking each series for you to understand the concept better.

➢ **Millionaire Wealth Principle 1**

Believe that you can create your life and not that life happens to you. In all ramifications, always hold yourself accountable for any action. Rich people have faith, and they are optimistic about life challenges. So, whenever you face any challenge, always keep the hope high, don't quit, or even settle for less.

Now, talking about the main takeaway for millionaire wealth principle 1, we have compiled the method to embrace that'd allow you to achieve your goal. These are some of the principles you'll need to accept as truth if you're going to become a millionaire. Without further ado, below are the principles to adopt.

Stop Blaming Yourself over Failure – When you want to develop the millionaire mindset, you have to follow this principle. Stop blaming yourself and instead accept the fact that the problems come your way. Moreover, you can see that as a challenge that'd make you strive.

Stop Justifying Yourself – In any situation, you may find yourself, stop justifying yourself. Say to yourself that you can achieve whatever you put your mind to without distraction from anyone. Be honest to yourself, and you shouldn't say that something is not important because you've not achieved the goal.

Stop Complaining and Focus on Action – One such thing to remember is to stop complaining and instead focus on action. If you lose money, there's no point blaming yourself. Stop complaining and do your due diligence because complaining after losing money won't get you back the money.

- **Millionaire Wealth Principle 2**

The millionaire wealth principle 2 involves using money to find more money. This means, as a rich man in making, you should always play the money game to win. It's only poor people that play money games not to lose. In all their games, they are always scared of losing, thereby allowing them to develop the confidence to win. Sometimes, they are afraid to risk the little money they have in possession of more income. So, set your potential income, in the long run, to become financially stable faster. Millionaire wealth principle 2 entails the following.

Set up a convenient goal that you can achieve.

Break down your long-term goals into smaller ones.

Always remember your long-term goals and strive hard to monitor your progress.

Re-evaluate and adjust the goal when necessary.

Eliminate the fear of starting if you have one.

Connect your long-term goals to your mentor.

Always avoid perfectionism by getting comfortable with uncertainty.

- **Millionaire Wealth Principle 3**

Always know that rich people are committed to being rich. So don't quit even when you're in tough times. It is only poor people that want to be rich without challenges. Besides, if we want to attract wealth, we must subconsciously desire to get it done. Getting rich takes focus, faith, time, and courage.

Aside from that, you'll need to develop a never-give-up attitude. Keep it in mind that millionaire wealth principle 3 is just like playing the lottery game every day. You'll have to develop the courage to win and achieve what you've been looking for in the long run. Without further ado, below are the things that principle 3 entails.

Exploit your skills to attain the goal.

Build a portfolio of getting rich like successful investors as they stay committed to their goals.

Stop procrastinating and know that there's no magic for success.

Create a budget and invest in yourself.

- **Millionaire Wealth Principle 4**

Another principle of developing a millionaire mindset is to think big. Remember, rich people, think big while poor people think small. So, the bigger you think, the bigger result you'll likely see. What you'll keep in mind is the quality of your thinking, your value, and the purpose of thinking like a millionaire.

Amazing Ways to Think Big

Write down your vision, close your eye and let your imagination do the work.

Think about scalability and train your brain to think big.

Take over the world and change the world mindset.

Surround with people that allow you to think better.

Study people, environment, prefer possible solutions when needed.

Turn off the noise and test the capacity of an idea.

☐ Let your idea loose without curiosity.

➢ **Millionaire Wealth Principle 5**

One of the principles to note is the millionaire wealth principle 5. Here, you'll have to believe that rich people focus on opportunities while poor people focus on obstacles. Also, focusing on potential growth and rewards could avoid you making choices based upon fear. So, remember the law of attraction as you move forward. In other words, if we focus on obstacles, we will attract obstacles in the future. So, it's better to face growth, practice optimism and whenever someone mentions a problem or obstacle, reframe it to succeed. Below are the ways to search for opportunities while thinking like a millionaire.

THINK LIKE A MILLIONAIRE

Be willing to read and research well on successful investors and entrepreneurs.

Meet like-minded folks, go for what you want, and take out a short quiz to know if you're on the right path.

Look at the big picture and look at industry trends and insight.

Live below your means and develop a written financial plan.

Get professional advice and invest in ways that work for you.

Furthermore, even if you're in debt, becoming a millionaire can often be a realistic goal. A lot of people may see this audacious goal but fail to achieve it. That's why we specifically emphasize financial temperament and responsibility. If you focus on luck alone to be a millionaire, you may go astray.

Moreover, there are few instances where one could become a millionaire through luck. Oftentimes, you'll need to have the financial discipline to be able to end up being successful. Some of the strategies to become a millionaire are easy to replicate but require timely effort. They include creating a financial plan, doing research on what you're about to do, establishing equity ownership, invest, re-invest, and diversify your investment for multiple streams of income.

Similarly, having a conservative-contrarian mindset is a great way to accomplish your goals. If everyone believes what you believe, and you're wrong, it might affect your goals. On the other hand, if nobody believes your thesis and contrarian, you might be telling the truth. So, work hard to make sure you're doing the right thing. Even in today's business environment, overnight success stories may happen.

Luck is certainly a component, and your driving force can allow you to attain the goals. That way, it's entirely up to you how hard you work to become a millionaire. People have overcome unthinkable obstacles, and you can as well do that. Whenever you have an experience of an economic downturn, don't panic. Instead, understand that there are tough times. So, take a bold step in your journey.

➢ Millionaire Trait that You Should Possess

Millionaires have several traits that make them unique from others. For some millionaires, striking it rich takes courage, while some will tell you that it's hard work and passion. Regardless of what makes them unique, we have compiled seven millionaire traits that'll guide you while thinking like a millionaire.

- Seeking Out Mentorship: Young millionaires seek out mentorship, and they are also smart enough to understand that they don't know it all. They recognize that there is a lot of value and experience. Besides, they put their ego aside and take time to seek out mentorship from successful millionaires in today's world.

- Creativity and Intuition: Thinking like a millionaire cannot make you rich without applying a millionaire's principles. Aside from that, you'll need to include creativity and intuition in whatever things you'll like to do that'd make you a millionaire. Follow the trend with your creativity and evolve with it and pay attention to your inner voice.

- Thriving on Knowledge: Not all young millionaires have a traditional education, so there's a need to thrive on knowledge. As an adage goes, knowledge is power, and you can't become a millionaire at any stage without knowledge. This way, dedication, commitment, and learning are especially important if you want to become a millionaire.

- Get Rid of Failure: As I have mentioned earlier in this book, fear of failure can make you not achieve the millionaire goal. One of the things that millionaires possess is the failure habit. They believe challenges will come and overcoming them is part of the things that'd make you become a millionaire. However, failure is an opportunity to learn and grow, so don't put yourself out there if you're not ready to fail in what you do.

- Always Focus on Your Strength: Forget trying to be the jack of all trades and instead focus on your strength. By focusing on your strength, you'll be able to achieve long-term goals. Here, you'll think about how to become a millionaire whether you want to invest in real estate, cryptocurrency, or other investment packages. Remember, no one has ever succeeded in doing what they are not good at. Therefore, build a team that motivates you and also focuses on your strength.

In summary of part one, we have talked about how to develop the millionaire mindset. Aside from that, you can also identify the 'you now vs. the future you.' From the explanation above, all you need is to develop the right mindset. Differentiate between what you want now and what you're capable of achieving in the nearest future. We have also explained some notable points that'd help you.

Nonetheless, diversify your portfolio and embrace the SWOT analysis. The acronym SWOT means Strength, Weaknesses, Opportunities, and Threats. Now, identify your strength, don't focus on your weaknesses as this may lead to failure. So, look for opportunities and the threat in-between to achieve a desirable result in the long run.

➢ Millionaire Signs

After following the description above, there are many signs that you'll become a millionaire. When you discover any of these signs, be sure to focus on your strength. This is because; you're halfway on the top of becoming a millionaire. Without further ado, below are the different signs that you'll become a millionaire.

- Having multiple streams of income. Having multiple streams of income is one of the signs that you'll become a millionaire someday. Don't just put your egg in one basket and instead create prior to making your first million through different investment packages.

- Surrounding yourself with like-minded folks. When you surround yourself with high-achieving people, you are just a bit closer to becoming a millionaire. This is because we definitely become rich like the people we associate with, and that's why winners are always attracted to winners.

- Being persistent and always talk about Ideas. Great minds always discuss ideas and not things. Remember that part of the principles of becoming a millionaire is to be creative. So, while the masses talk about cars and movies, millionaires talk about ideas and several things that could make them become successful now and in the future.

- Being comfortable taking risks. Another sign that you'll become a millionaire is when you're comfortable taking calculated risks. Millionaires overcome fears and instead educate themselves to take calculated risks that would likely shape their lives. More so, when you think big, you'll definitely want to take calculated risk as no one would ever strike rich without huge expectations.

Part Two: Increasing Your Income

Chapter 5: Making Something from Nothing

Being a successful entrepreneur is just akin to being a magician. For instance, you started from scratch, and one minute, you're rich. Do you want to live for that magic? If yes, you're on the right track. More so, twenty years ago, there's nothing like Bitcoin, but today the innovative Omni-channel has shifted beyond the status quo to diversify individual investment portfolios in recent times. Now, everyone wants to invest in cryptocurrency as it is a groundbreaking technology and one of the largest cryptocurrencies that people invest in.

What makes a magician so appealing are the effortless traits? To make something out of nothing could somewhat be magic if you follow the right path. Perhaps, one needs to put in hard work, smart work, genuineness, and innovative mindset possession. Your talent, aptitude, and connections can also help you along the line. But, most importantly, you have to create the desire to create something and watch it flourish.

However, this magic is what could make you achieve your goal. Besides, there are tons of hidden secrets that successful investors won't tell you about making something from anything. Have you gone through the stories of successful billionaires like Oprah Winfrey, Howard Schultz, Ralph Lauren, Harold Hamm, and many others who grew up poor? Well, with this, you'll know that you don't have to be born with a silver spoon to become great in life. Whether you need inspiration or want to start a business, you need to know how these folks made it to the top. No matter how ambitious, driven, or disciplined you are, you can definitely achieve what you set your mind to. Forget about the worries and challenges that'd come your way. All you need to focus on is how you can achieve these goals and make something out of nothing. According to CNBC, the good news now is that you're not too late to become a success story. Thousands of ordinary people became millionaires today. This way, how much you'll make doesn't matter but to be successful like other investors in today's world.

➢ Steps to Wealth Creation

Upon turning from a poor man to a successful/wealthy man, there are many things to consider. First, you need to understand what success means to you. After that, seek knowledge, and follow your dream. We are going to start by highlighting the steps to wealth creation. Below are the five steps to consider.

- **Be Creative**

Creativity is one of the first things to embrace a new life. Besides, always know that to be creative, you'll have to believe that you're creative. Moreover, learn to observe, listen, and explore the innovative world to be productive. Talk to your friends, be aware of things and bring out ideas to wealth creation.

Meanwhile, know the problem you're solving. Identifying the problem may somewhat require a daunting process. But figure out the cure to a life-changing environment and persistent problems of the past. With this, you'll be able to achieve your goal, thereby creating wealth from a zero background to networking.

- **Make Reading Your Priority**

Reading allows you to imbibe the traits of successful investors. While reading, make sure you put everything you've read into practice. Not every leader is the same, so select the ones that match your personality or go in line with your set goals and objectives. Besides, reading is to the brain, and you can only achieve your goal by implementing what's in your brain. After all, you're creating something that'd generate value for another organization.

- **Get the Right Mindset**

Part of what could make you develop the SMART goal, as stated in part one of this book, is to have the right mindset. Without optimism, you're going nowhere. That's why; I'll advise you to embrace the SMART goal with the right attitude. Thinking is essential for facing challenges; so, explore your experience of the world around you with the right mindset and see previous notes regarding the SMART acronym to understand what it entails.

- **Move towards Achieving Goal**

Since you're planning to make something work out of nothing, you have to be committed. No one is going to motivate unless you move and inspire yourself to achieve the goal. Also, don't let the notion of inclement weather dull your spirit. Instead, look for something that'd allow you to move closer to the goal. Moreover, a positive attitude is at the heart of creative endeavors to be successful. If possible, make the process fun, be curious when there are obstacles, and you're halfway towards making something work.

- **Search for Investment Opportunities**

Searching for investment opportunities is another way to make something from nothing. Read success stories of Elon Musk, Jeff Bezos, Bill Gates, and many other successful entrepreneurs. With that, you'll know that investment can elevate your riches or create a success story for you in the long run.

In today's 21st century, there are many kinds of investments you can engage in. while trying to do that, be aware that they are not a get-rich scheme. So, be ready to invest in the long-term to achieve an attainable goal. Without further ado, let's walk you through some investment types that could drive you out to become successful in today's world.

Real Estate Investment – Real estate investment is among the things that could help you build bountiful wealth in the long run. The world we live in today is a digital one, and searching for a home has been one of the world's major things. So, here's an opportunity to apply the buy-and-hold strategy for long-term profit.

Cryptocurrency: Cryptocurrency has been confirmed to have the potentials to enable social and economic growth throughout the world. Since it's a digital currency that has no government interference, one can invest and make a huge profit with time. You can research and select the one that you think is the best for you. Nonetheless, Bitcoin has surpassed other cryptos, and this could create a success story for you.

Stock and Shares Investment: Stock and shares investment has continued to deliver generous returns to investors. If you want to make something out of nothing, this is also another chance. As the country grows, you can take care of the growing economy. Also, it is the best way to stay ahead of inflation and earn money in cool ways. Besides, they are easy to buy and also easy to sell whether the time is right.

Government Bonds Investment

Government bonds investment is a debt security issued by the government to support spending. They are considered a low-risk investment because the return on investment or the interest is low compared to other forms of investment. The logic behind this investment option is that the government seeks out money from investors to raise money for projects or day-to-day operations.

Freelancing and Blog Creation

The Internet has made it easy for students and young folks to make something out of nothing in this modern world. With the help of

Upwork, Fiverr, and other freelance workspaces, you can even become a millionaire in no time. The creation of blogs is also an important factor in wealth creation.

To start making money as a blogger, there are many things to consider. Part of which includes promoting your blog, a good knowledge of Search Engine Optimization (SEO), and many others. If you'd love to make something out of nothing through blogging, we have compiled the steps needed for blog creation.

Steps Needed for Blog Creation

Whether you're starting from scratch or you're a writer, it makes perfect sense. You can use a blog to sell yourself to the public. With your name, you can be famous, thereby achieving your desired goals. More so, blogging is a great way to experiment with your writing style in unique ways. Without further ado, take a look at the steps to start a new blog below.

Select a domain name and check whether it's available to chase.

Purchase a hosting package from a rightful source and install WordPress.

Pick a theme and your blog header.

Write your blog page and install plugins/widgets.

Promote your page and start earning.

Chapter 6: Starting up A Business.

Did you know that you can grow from nothing to something by starting a business? Well, starting a business involves planning, making financial decisions, conducting market research, and completing a series of legal activities. It is a huge commitment that has a lot of obstacles while growing the business.

That way, you commit yourself to think like a millionaire, highlighting your plan first. Do you want to start a business, or would you invest in becoming a millionaire? These are the questions you'll need to provide answers to before venturing into starting a business in today's digital world.

To be realistic, it is 100 percent possible to start your own business. The only thing that could hinder you is that starting a business takes time to grow. Aside from that, it requires endless effort and a potentially few setback. Your commitment and determination are what put you through the challenges in due time.

At this point, there's a need to know how to start a business. Why do you think people do endless research before starting a business? Whether it's a small-scale retail business or a large-scale one, planning is essential when it comes to starting a business. Does it make sense to apply for a loan to start a business?

Of course, it makes sense, but it can be somewhat difficult to know the right steps to take. Also, know that starting a business is a trial-and-error process. You win some, and you may lose some cash during the course of running the business. So, don't be overwhelmed with the decision to start but rather begin the process. To get you started your new business, there are lots of things to put in place.

➢ Step-By-Step Guide to Starting A Business

Tasks like naming the business and creating a logo may be quite daunting. Whether it is determining your business structure or crafting a different market strategy, the workload can be somewhat challenging as well. That way, check out these step-by-step guides to transform your business from a lightbulb to reality.

- Define Your Why and Refine your idea.

One of the key factors to consider while starting a business is to know your purpose. It is good to know why you're launching your business. This is because; you'll definitely want to go with the person why or a marketplace why. The scope of the business is vital, and you'll also need to design your personal needs. In other words, do quick research for existing companies in your field to know where you stand.

- Brainstorm a Suitable Business Name

Business name is the first thing people consider before checking out what you sell. So, before nailing down your ideas, understand the reasoning behind those ideas. This means that you'll need to brainstorm a suitable business name that will attract potential customers. Regardless of which option you choose, check whether the business name is good enough to disclose to the public.

- Write Your Business Plan

Once you have an idea of what kind of business you want to start, it's crucial to write a business plan. Besides, know the purpose of your business. Aside from that, identify your target audience and how you will finance your start-up cost. Meanwhile, don't rush into starting a business without pondering down your needs. A lot of mistakes are made by new start-ups, and this can make the company fold up.

- Conduct Market Research and Exit Strategy

Conducting thorough market research on your field or area of specialization is an important part of crafting a business plan. Besides, market research and exit strategy help you know your target audience, their needs, competitors, and behaviors to a particular product. On the flip side, knowing when to quit doing the wrong thing helps you figure out where the company is going. When there are losses, these market research and exit strategies can help you to sustain them.

- Always Perform A Break-Even Analysis

A break-even analysis allows you to know what you're up to in the industry. Once you can get your start-up capital, break-even analysis helps with the breakdown of profits in the future. With the help of this analysis, you can reduce the chance of getting losses during the cost of running your investment. The break-even analysis has a formula; fixed assets divided by average price minus variable cost.

Reasons Why Break-even Analysis is Essential

To generally determine profitability in the long run

When you think about selling your product, break-even analysis help with pricing.

You can analyze your company's data to track your progress with the break-even analysis.

Break-even analysis also monitors and control cost.

It saves time and frustration of growing your business.

➢ Why Starting Up a Business Can Make You a Millionaire?

Kicking off the millionaire mindset by starting up a business can make you successful. Confusion and doubt may weigh you down, but how do you begin the process? By having the right mindset, you're halfway to achieving the goal. In fact, successful millionaires tend to set up their own businesses today.

We-you and me- have all been lied to about the challenges in starting a business. To be successful, you have to look beyond the challenges. Why do you think successful millionaires own their businesses today? Not to worry, the secret behind becoming a millionaire is to focus on growing your business.

Yes! Transformational success requires radical change. This way, you'll need to learn how to start something new. According to a Forbes survey, 99.9 percent of entrepreneurs today sacrifice their time to create something from nothing. They fight anxiety for years to decades, and this made them become successful millionaires.

Why do you think most entrepreneurs' live lives of quiet desperation? Well, this is because; they are worried about being successful. How to start, run, and grow a business may be challenging at first, but the urge to become a millionaire can change your mindset. Billions are spent by training, reading, and many speakers can even convince you to increase your spending to grow faster and become a millionaire.

However, getting rich begins with the right mindset. Steve Siebold, a self-made millionaire, discloses that many people don't understand the nature of building wealth. If your parents were broke or in the middle class, you might end up being broke if you follow their philosophies about money. While the masses believe that becoming wealthy is for the rich men, you really need to think beyond the fact.

The secret has been the same long ago. It's no difference, and in fact, it's not a new thing to start up a business. Change the cause, be grateful for what you have, and use it to incur future wealth. So, ultimately, you'll become what you desire without a lottery, inherit money but the result of smart work.

There are tons of reasons why starting up a business can make you a millionaire in the nearest future. If you're able to study successful people in the world, you'll know that they start up a business to become successful. Without much talk, below are the reasons why starting a business could make you achieve your goal of becoming a millionaire.

It allows you to join the fast-growing company in the world.

Starting up a business allow you to become a specialist in a particular field.

In most cases, it exposes you to creativity and formal education.

You can secure a management position and join other fast-growing start-ups.

Starting a business is a frugal and slow way to wealth.

It increases your earning potentials in the long run, thereby making you a millionaire.

You will become financially literate and be able to protect yourself from loss.

➤ Things to Do Before Starting a Business

It's most likely possible that you'll find a competitor in whatever business you want to start. Understanding the work involved and making proper planning will help you during the process. Aside from that, you should know that starting a business can be stressful. It often feels like completing different tasks at the same time, but in reality, with little planning, you can be a successful owner.

Beyond giving it your all, it's crucial that you know the seven things needed to start a business. Be realistic about the risk involved, understand the timing, hire help when necessary, and follow the step-by-step guide listed above. Experts say some good seven things to do before starting a business are.

Spend Time Considering Your Audience

Always know that you cannot start a business without knowing your target audience. This is because; they are the driving force in each decision you make. So, spend time understanding the people that need your product or service. Part of this movement is to know whether you're going to be a business-to-business (B2B) or a business-to-consumer (B2C) enterprise. Within these parameters are multiple categories. Therefore, know the age limit of people that want your service or product, gender, and even profession.

Know Your Business Purpose and Have a Strong Mission

You can't become a millionaire without knowing your business purpose. By recognizing your business strength, you'll be able to expand your services to reach a larger audience. Besides, understanding your purpose and having a strong mission clearly defined your existence and how impactful you are to the world.

Standing out among competitors is no easy feat, and the magic behind winning is to have a mission.

Map Your Finances and Choose a Structure

Starting a business requires money and planning, as we've said earlier. So, to be successful and be able to become a millionaire, you'll need to seek out ways to acquire capital. Apart from seeking out funds, spending it right is also vital. However, there are plenty of options available to map your finances. At the same time, choose the structure to which your company will operate. Here, you'll decide whether your company needs to employ someone to achieve your goal, or you'll have to run the business alone.

Calculate the Risk Involved

Of course, there will always be a level of risk in the process of running your business. Calculating, understanding, and planning for risk are important steps to take before starting your business. This means you need to access your business risk and know what it takes before writing a business plan. More so, be honest with yourself about the risk, as this can help protect your new business in due time.

Be Able to Manage your Expectations

No matter how good your idea is, everything may not work as planned. So, you need to manage your expectations to see profits. Whatever your plan may be, always manage your expectations to avoid disappointment. So, stay strong and be optimistic when things are not going the way you want them.

Be an Expert in Your Field

Often, many entrepreneurs will tell you they learn what they know from experience. Truth be told, many of them are experts in their chosen field. So, when you're looking to start a new business, know the full details of the business before starting. The more you know, the better chance of becoming a millionaire in the long run.

Be Passionate About Your Work

If you are starting a business, you have to be ready to work and work. According to most entrepreneurs, the first 3 years of starting your company may be quite challenging. (Forbes) So, be ready for it and be passionate. This is because; being passionate is one of the things that would make you successful in the business you've set up.

➢ Mistakes to Avoid When Starting a Business

According to business experts, there are many mistakes to avoid when it comes to starting a business. Moreover, 20 percent of new business fails during the first two years of starting the business. (Forbes statistics 2019) We've reached out to many business experts and the stories of successful entrepreneurs in today's world.

However, we will walk you through the seven mistakes to avoid when starting a business. Anyone of the mistakes listed below can sabotage your new business venture and turn it into a failure. While there's a foolproof plan to reach a business start-up, avoiding the following mistakes can make you achieve your goal.

- Not Working in SMART Direction

    Goals can give you different directions when you first start your business. However, working on your SMART goal is a crucial way to achieve these goals. On the other hand, if you're not working in a SMART direction, achieving these goals may require a daunting process. Therefore, identify where you want to go and know your purpose.

- Avoid Partnering with the Wrong Investors

    One important piece of advice that you should consider when starting a business is to avoid partnering with the wrong person. Since you've placed your confidence in your business potentials, partnering with the wrong person may lead you astray. So, check your partner whether you both possess the right mindset.

- Don't undervalue Your Product.

    When you're starting your business, don't undervalue your product or service. Successful investors and manufacturers start with the best intentions of giving their services or products for free. Moreover, you have to be careful while doing this because the process might ruin your company in the long run. Also, don't launch your product too quickly. Besides, make sure your systems and processes are in place.

- Create a Detailed Marketing Strategy

If you've read the stories of successful investors, you'll truly understand that they became successful by creating a detailed marketing plan. If you have successfully validated the problem, market your start-up as this will help you get more users. Don't hire the wrong person to do this for you because different skillsets and backgrounds are needed to create a strong marketing plan.

- Overspending and Underspending

Starting a business doesn't have to require a huge sum of money, but some business owners need to spend money to purchase the right tools. While doing this, avoid overspending on irrelevant material that won't be beneficial in the long run. Perhaps, avoid underspending in order not to fall on the other end of the spectrum. Starting and growing a business with limited funds may hinder your progress.

- Not Being Committed to Achieving Success

Remember, one of the first things to become a millionaire is to stay committed to it. Not being committed to your goal may bring the business down. Moreover, starting a business requires a number of success-oriented traits, dedication, and a sense of commitment. So, be committed to having the right millionaire mindset and remain resilient when you make a mistake to allow success to be within your reach.

- Choosing the Wrong Business Structure

If you choose the wrong business structure, you might not achieve your business goals. In fact, it may lead you astray in getting the millionaire dream. So, do further research, register your business with the right legal entity to avoid problems in the long run. However, choosing the best business structure may be quite daunting. But, when you seek the knowledge of experts in your area of expertise, getting the right business structure would be easy, thereby making you become a millionaire in the long run.

Chapter 7: Building Passive Income Streams

Passive income is referred to as any money you earn in a manner that doesn't require much effort. Surprisingly, while you're asleep, you can be earning passive incomes. Aside from that, if you're industrious and innovative, you can earn money through passive income streams in today's world.

Speaking from experience, adding passive income to your investment portfolio is a great way to accelerate your financial goal to become a millionaire. For example, getting started with real estate or cryptocurrency investment with just $1,000 can increase your income and your other investment goals.

But deep down inside, you know you've always wanted to become a millionaire. With this in mind, multiple streams of income shouldn't be an option but a necessity. You've probably heard of active income, right? In theory, we will differentiate the two terms and how passive income is essential.

➢ **Active Income vs. Passive Income – Which One Is Suitable?**

In a simple explanation, active income refers to the income you earn for the service you perform. It includes wages, salaries, commissions, and other remunerations received from performing a task. Depending on your financial and occupational situation, active income may require skills. In fact, you can either work as a full-time, a part-time, or contractual worker for being an active income earner.

However, having regular active income has distinct advantages and disadvantages. For one, it is more predictable and secure. On the other hand, you can be denied your salary in a couple of months due to the inability to meet your key performance indicator (KPI) or other notable or suspicious reasons. Passive income is quite different and unique in its ways. It describes the idea of starting a business and making money work for you. Now, how do you earn through passive income?

There are many ways to earn through passive income. Not to rush; we will definitely walk you through the process. But before that, know that some passive income streams may be lucrative and also require payment on a monthly basis. Besides, they have inherent risk, and this is one thing that makes it unique from the active income of 9 am-5 pm work ethics. Meanwhile, you can take advantage of both incomes.

Alternatively, the more you earn from passive income, the more you forget about the active ones. In fact, one financial goal you can set is to earn through multiple streams of passive income in today's digital world. All that said, an understanding of the relationship between the two terms is essential. Having both active and passive income will open possibilities and opportunities to become a millionaire.

Whether you're trying to save up for something special or want to start a business, building an empire of passive income is something that could help you achieve the goal. This is because; Forbes magazine disclosed that an average millionaire is estimated to have more than five streams of income. Be a positive thinker and have the right mindset that'd give you enough financial freedom you always wanted to be in the future.

Some income may come from the investment you've made. So, why not have multiple investment portfolios to build wealth? Most of us are familiar with active income, yet we refused to diversify and explore. In this 21st century, you'll have to be innovative and also evolve to achieve your desired goals and objectives. Remember, you want to become a millionaire, so you shouldn't stop exploring.

➢ How to Shift Your Livelihood to Passive Income

Don't go by the philosophy that all wealth is created through active income. If this statement was true, successful investors like Warren Buffett, Carl Icahn, Carlos Slim, Elon Musk, and many others wouldn't have made it to the top. Active income can only help you secure a fixed income in the long run.

Nevertheless, not all passive income is created to make you rich. To clarify, passive incomes are safe, stable, and can relieve you from financial burden. When you reach the stage in your life when you no longer think about working, you should know that you've changed your livelihood to passive income.

Unfortunately, only a few people know how to get to this stage in life. That's why this book is a guide to becoming a millionaire. With sincerity and pure honesty, you can't read this book without changing your mindset towards becoming a millionaire. However, most people are just investing, hoping to have a solid passive income someday. That's not how to be successful, rather research more to be wealthy.

Now, how do you shift your livelihood to passive income? The answer is simple, and it is categorized in threefold. The first thing you need is to identify your passive income profile. Know the right thing to invest your hard-earned money on. Secondly, avoid getting a fixed income, and the third thing to consider is to be innovative and creative towards achieving your goals and objectives today.

➢ Stages to Solid Passive Incomes Today

To build passive income streams, there are five stages you'll need to understand. With the knowledge of these stages, you don't have to rack your brain to be successful. Since one of the major roadblocks to financial freedom is to have one source of income, you need to explore multiple streams of income.

To create multiple streams, you must come with a growth mindset. So, you'll know that to be successful in passive income requires time and perseverance. Without further ado, below are the five stages to solid passive income.

- **Stage 1 – Regular Income Earner**

Always know that all passive incomes are created from active income. Thus, the more active income you have accumulated, the more passive income you can create in due time. (James Royal, investor and Wealth Management at Bankrate). Also, spending time on investing your active income is a crucial factor in delaying financial freedom. Therefore, you can become a regular income earner if you kick your investment portfolio with a large amount of active income.

- **Stage 2 – Saver Stage**

To build solid passive income, you'll have to save a huge amount of money to invest for long-term profit. Saving is critical for investing, and it is the seed to attain financial freedom. If you cannot save to invest on multiple passive incomes, the seed of greatness is not in you. In fact, you may not be able to achieve your millionaire goals. Therefore, if you want to build a passive income, you must make investment a priority.

- **Stage 3 – Income Loss Emergency Protection**

This third stage emphasizes protecting yourself against sudden income loss. With the help of income loss emergency protection, you'll always maintain your financial stability and track your progress. If you want to build passive income, an emergency protection fund is crucial. You can create this fund or open an account with any bank and state your terms and conditions. This means that you'll have to keep a certain amount of money aside to be able to withstand losses in the process of your investment.

- **Stage 4 – Cash Reserve Builder**

    After you might have applied the income loss emergency protection, there's a need to build some cash in reserve. This allows you to be free from financial distractions. Having a cash reserve is essential as it helps investors engage in short-term and long-term passive income. In a simple term, a typical amount to keep in reserve should be at least $2,500 to $5,000. (Forbes) You're wondering how you can make this possible, right. Yes! Since you're just starting to become a millionaire, keep at least 5 percent of your start-up capital aside to serve as your cash reserve.

- **Stage 5 – Passive income Investing.**

    The fifth stage is the passive income investing stage that allows you to build assets. Choose the right passive income investment package. Whenever you're in your investment journey, always take a step that would lead to your success and move you towards achieving your goals. So, now that you know the five stages to build solid passive income; let's explain the types of passive income in today's world.

➤ **Smart Passive Income Ideas Millionaires' Need**

It's no doubt that there are tons of passive incomes that can make you a millionaire. Without an income stream, your business may not grow. So, having multiple streams of income is a good way of safeguarding your business against a downturn. Besides, it can give your business stability, allowing you to achieve your goals and objectives. To manage this effectively, below are the smart passive income ideas today. We have discussed these extensively in the previous chapters.

Real Estate Investment

Buying Dividend-paying Shares

Government Bonds

Other passive income ideas, when applied strategically, can help you stack your way to millions.

Affiliate Marketing/networking

Cashback sites and storage rentals

Investing in a real estate investment trust

Refinancing your mortgage

Peer to Peer lending/Licensing music

Chapter 8: Adding a Side Hustle to your 9-5 Job

The truth is most 9 to 5 jobs cannot pay your bills. Especially if you're just starting your career, the process can be quite daunting. When you calculate the cost of food, transportation, bills, and more, you will realize that you barely have anything leftover. Now, why do you think side hustle is the solution?

Well, side hustles are the jobs that allow you to make money outside your 9 to 5 job. They allow you to buy things you need and make you have lower financial worries. As said by CNBC, 9 to 5 jobs may increase your salaries by 5 percent, but can that solve your problem? No! So starting a side hustle to make an extra hundred dollars is vital and can go a long way today. Let's quickly dive into how to develop a successful side hustle.

➢ **How to Develop Side Hustles**

So, you have decided to start a side hustle but don't know how it works. Relax, as we have a list of steps to follow while developing side hustles. Also, keep in mind that while adding these side hustles to your 9 to 5 jobs, you can work as much or as little as you'd like since there's no distraction from a third party.

Make a list of what you're passionate about

Decide if you'd invest in real estate, cryptocurrency, or other investment types.

Schedule time for your side hustles and make sure there are no conflicts of interest.

Put 65 percent of your energy into your day job and commit yourself with 35 percent side hustle.

Validate your side hustles with incredible customers.

Define clear goals and set milestones that'll force you to progress.

Ask for customer's feedback and delegate work outside of your expertise.

Re-engage yourself and avoid getting fired from your day job.

Build a sustainable flow of income.

Think of your regular employment as you test the viability of the side hustle.

➤ How to Effectively Build a Side Hustle

Time Management

It is a huge myth that you have to spend up to 15 to 30 hours on your side hustle. Besides, you can set a negotiable time to work on your project. If you don't have enough time to complete your project, chip it away and find a visible opportunity that won't interrupt the 15 to 30 hours block of time you set. This means that you will have to set a time to balance the working hours between your side hustle and normal work hours.

Be Clear About Your Mission

This also constitutes another tip on how to effectively build a side hustle while running your 9 to 5 job. Be clear about the reasons for starting the side hustles. Not everyone wants to leave their full-time jobs for side hustles. So, do you want to pay off debt, saving for an emergency fund, or you're saving for a home down payment? These are the questions you'll need to provide answers to effectively build a side hustle.

Find the Right One

Finding the right-side hustle is one of the criteria to become successful. This might seem like an impossible goal, but when you take the time to find the right one, you'll have a strong foundation to succeed. Moreover, determine your strongest skills, and look at your previous experience to create one.

Get Rid of Distractions

We live in a distracted world today where social media and other addictive apps are vying for attention. To stay focused and effectively build a side hustle, you need to eliminate distractions. It's easier said than done, and you may be tempted but always remember the dream to become a millionaire to keep you going.

Leverage Teamwork Collaboration/Joint Forces

Many people start their side hustles on their own, but yours can be different. Besides, there may come a time when you'll need to manage the side hustle for expansion. In this case, you need to seek the opinions of others in your area of expertise to keep the momentum going. So, when you reach that point in your life, don't be afraid to ask for help.

Part Three: Saving & Investing

Chapter 9: Emergency Fund

Alvin and Dara's long-term goal was to raise $10,000 to buy a house. They both have good jobs, and to reduce costs, they have agreed to drive reliable old cars. With good pay and low cost, they could deposit $500 a month into a financial market deposit account. Interestingly, these monthly savings will allow them to save at a low cost and buy their home in 24 months.

But one cold morning, one of their cars didn't start. It's time to buy a new battery, which costs $52; with this unexpected cost, Alvin and Dara could save only $448 that month. Undeterred, the following month, they resumed their savings plan. There were other expenses: dental hygiene, some unplanned high costs, and an emergency trip to see Dara's mother, who was ill. Each time, they used their savings to pay off their expenses, and the following month they saved another $500. They were able to buy their home a few months later.

If you were in Alvin and Dara's shoes, would you have expected an unexpected expense?

Emergencies can swallow your money and send your family into financial trouble. Even small expenses like cell phones falling into the water, vet bills when a dog eats something unhealthy, and helping a friend or family member in need or family can ruin your monthly budget.

➢ What Is an Emergency Fund?

Don't think of your emergency fund as your regular savings account. For example, you can make plans for your home insurance, car insurance deductions, and everyday medical expenses. An emergency fund comes when something unexpected happens, it helps you get out of trouble.

➢ Reasons You Need an Emergency Fund

In a Federal Reserve test, only 48 percent of respondents said they could pay $400 without borrowing or selling something. Some studies suggest that households with emergency savings of less than $500 may be more prone to anxiety, sleep deprivation, and other side effects than home-saving.

Your emergency fund will cover you in the event of an unexpected bankruptcy or job loss and can help you avoid getting into debt. It can help you maintain a relaxed state should it be you fall sick or have a large car or home repair that you wouldn't be able to afford. But there are a lot of reasons you need to work to increase your emergency fund. Learn about them here:

To help pay off debt quickly and easily.

Your emergency fund is a significant factor in your finances. You can use it to clear off unexpected bills at any time. For example, when you're on the road, you could effortlessly pay your car repairs or medical bills. Use your emergency fund to handle these crazy events and make it easier for you to stay focused on getting out of debt.

It's easy to go into debt when you have an incredible amount of bills.

You have started a budget.

When you start a budget, you may lose track of some of the expenses you need to plan. Your emergency fund may cover some of the costs for the first year, after which you can add those costs to the budget as they arise.

This could be annual expenses such as taxes or other items such as gifts or party fees. Your emergency fund can help you adjust your budget.

As unplanned expenses arise, write them down and adjust your budget to enable you to make better plans in the future.

After a few months, you should have no unexpected expenses.

You only have one source of income.

If you have one source of income in your household, having an emergency fund is important. This can help you to avoid unexpected job losses or illnesses that prevent the breadwinner from working.

If you are a small family or still single, you should have one year of expenses in the emergency fund. You have better chances if you are still single to build your emergency fund as fast as you can.

You are self-employed.

If you work for yourself or, perhaps, you do a job that does not allow you access to benefits when you stop working or aren't employed, then you should consider setting up an emergency fund.

Additionally, if you know that you might stop working soon, you shouldn't hesitate to put more money into your emergency fund account.

To keep up with your home maintenance.

When you own a home, you must do some necessary repairs and upkeep. Although you might have set up a sinking fund to cover the cost for repairing and restructuring, unexpected expenses might arise such as plumbing repair, HVAC servicing, etc., that would cost you extra money. repair or air conditioning repairs.

Your emergency fund can help you set off these bills and make owning a home just less stressful. So, try setting up an emergency fund to save for these expenses before they occur. Remember to add tax payment to your budgeting too,

You have medical issues.

Having a serious illness can make you always spend more than you have planned. For instance, you might need to visit the hospital regularly for checkups, routine tests, or even take sick leave from your place of work. Having an emergency fund in place can help you deal with these unnecessary expenses, especially during challenging moments.

You're saving for a goal.

If you are looking forward to starting a business or buying a property, your emergency fund can stop you from dipping into your savings when unexpected expenses occur.

Although your goal for building your emergency fund account might slow down due to certain unpredictable reasons, you will be certain that your savings for other important goals won't be affected. It's a great way to protect your other kinds of savings.

Assess your emergency savings. If you do not have at least $500 on hand, go back to the income generation section in Part Two and learn to start up a side hustle to raise your emergency fund.

If you are single, work on building your emergency fund as soon as possible.

➤ Steps to Help You Grow Your Emergency Fund Faster

Do you want to reach your saving goals faster than expected? Then, you should try these expert-approved strategies to speed up your journey.

- Replacing luxury items with some of the lower-cost ones

Be your barista with an inexpensive homemade coffee machine. Or avoid the spa and try some particular homemade treatments instead.

- Sell your possessions with money.

Take a good look around your home for things you don't use or for items that cost you money. Selling those products will clean up the clutter and the emergency fund platform.

- Increase your earnings.

Even if it's temporary, make efforts to increase your income and accelerate your savings. You could try to do an extra shift or start additional work to earn more money.

- Take advantage of your windfalls.

Save at least some (or all) of your bonuses, commissions, tax returns, and credit card cashback.

➤ Where Do I Put My Emergency Fund?

When choosing an account with emergency funds, keep these three principles in mind; you want the money to be liquid, affordable, and free from market risk. A savings account is a great option to save your emergency money. You will need an FDIC (Federal Deposit Insurance Corporation)-protected bank account or an NCUSIF (National Credit Union Share Insurance Fund)-protected credit union account. Top experts advise that you separate your emergency fund from your regular savings. You can put the fund in a special account and use them only when needed.

➤ How Much Should I Save?

I recommend setting aside an average living expense of three to six months. To find that number, keep in mind that if you find yourself thrown into a crisis, the expenses you have (maybe less than what you usually spend) will reduce unnecessary expenses. To calculate what you might need for an emergency fund:

1. Divide your monthly expenses into three categories: needs, wants, and wishes.

2. Add the costs for the things you really can't do without - like mortgages or rent, food, gas, and electricity.

3. Take that number and multiply it by the number of days or weeks you want to contribute to the emergency fund.

For most people, that final cost can amount to tens of thousands. Consider working with a trusted financial professional to help you focus on your goals. And be sure to re-evaluate that number at least once a year. Your financial needs change over time. So, a new home, a new baby, or a job can have an immense impact on your emergency budget.

➢ Overcoming Obstacles When Saving for an Emergency Fund

For many people, just starting with an emergency fund may seem like too much money to save. But experts agree: The number one way to progress with your emergency fund is to turn your savings directly into a budget. Treat it like a bill; you must commit to saving a specific amount of money each month. But keep that amount in perspective. The key is to establish a fixed payment schedule. Decide ahead of time what your emergency fund contributions will look like to reach your goal. As a general rule of thumb, save 15 percent of your income towards your savings goals altogether. These can include internal payments, holiday gifts, new car brakes, and more. Organize your list of goals and determine how much of that 15 percent you will contribute to your emergency fund. Now, set up your accounts so that the savings contribution occurs automatically.

Schedule repeat bank transfers to transfer money to the emergency fund every month. With continued financial support and the power of combined interest, your balance will gradually increase. It would be best if you understood that there are bumps in the road, and people who will be successful in life have planned for uncertainty. So, start saving now. When something surprising happens, you should remain calm and take the time to sort it out.

Chapter 10: Think of Retirement

There is no better time to start thinking about retirement than now. Oh, yes. RIGHT NOW! The earlier you start saving and investing, the longer your savings will grow and reach what you will need to survive when you retire. But that's not the only reason why it's best to start saving early.

During your lifetime, there will always be an excuse to delay saving for your retirement. Whether it's because you want to pay off a student loan, you think you won't be making a lot of money compared to now, you want to buy a house, renovate a kitchen, have children, buy a car ... and an endless list of opportunities will follow. Life, with all its expenses, will not go unnoticed. So, you had better declare a full-stop and define the time to save for retirement!

The sooner you decide, the easier it will be to improve your saving habit. Of course, there may be times when you are not very careful at all, but every little thing counts. And those little bits you save, whether they're set to 401k or IRA, will be invested and recovered over the years. The money you save or invest when you are 50 years old will have less time to earn you a good ROI (Return on investment) than the money you save or invest when you are 25 years old.

Aside from the money aspect, you'll want to start thinking about what to do in retirement. Do you like to travel the world, play golf, take courses, learn to sew? One way to start is by asking yourself what you don't have time to do now. These are the activities you might want to do when you retire. It's essential to think about these things ahead of time, not only so you can have some guidance when the time comes but also to plan for any additional costs. What you do when you retire will affect how much you will need for your annual income and how much you will need to save for your anticipated lifestyle or hobbies.

➢ Finding Out How Much You Will Need

This is a million-dollar question.

Unfortunately, no answer has been established. The amount you will need will depend on your expenses in retirement. If, for example, you no longer have a mortgage or rent in retirement, you may be able to live on a lot less than if you continue to make those payments. On the other hand, if you live in an old house when you retire, you may receive more repairs than the new condo.

➢ Finding Ways to Set Money Aside Now

People delay saving for retirement because they think they will have more time to do so later. Another popular reason for putting it off is that most people don't know how to get the money they will save. However, if you read part 2 of this special guide, you can find different ways to earn money each month to save for retirement. Now let's explore the following sections to find specific ways to save more for retirement.

THINK LIKE A MILLIONAIRE

Food budgeting

If you eat take-out twice a week and pay $12 for a meal that would cost about $3.50 if you had prepared it at home, you could save about $72 a month in your retirement savings. Over 20 years at 5 percent, it's $ 33,266.94.

Cut your budget for clothes and shoes in half.

If you spend $ 1,000 a year on clothes and shoes, can you cut it in half and put $ 500 a year ($ 42 a month) in your retirement account? Thirty years with that at 6 percent, and you'll have $ 42,189.63 to retire.

Move to a smaller house.

If you now live with two other people in 2,400 square feet, would you move into a 1,800 square foot house and stay comfortable? If so, your mortgage payments can drop from $1,000 to $300 a month, which you can put into a retirement fund. In just fifteen years at 6 percent, a savings of $600 a month would equal $157,382.85.

Drive your car twice as long.

If you usually get a new car every three years, you should try something different. Instead, pay for your vehicle in three years but drive it for six. Deposit the extra amount that you would have used to purchase another car for the next three years into your retirement account. You will not only have contributed to your retirement account for three years out of every six but would have discovered a smarter way to save.

Pay off your loan.

One way to earn more money in retirement is to improve your mortgage when interest rates drop. With the cost of closing the loan, you can get another $50-$150 per month for your retirement savings. Don't just increase the length of the loan; otherwise, you will sacrifice your long-term financial health.

Start a temporary business.

Rather than just considering the potential costs of cuts, consider working a few hours a week, perhaps in your own business (see part 2 of this guide), and put that income into your retirement savings.

➤ Analyzing Tax-Deferred Ways to Save

Using America as a case study, when most people think of retiring and the government simultaneously, they think of Social Security. This government program collects money from you while still very active and working and pays it back to you, month by month, upon retirement.

If you are close to retirement, you can count on a small number of retirement benefits from Social Security. If you don't have one, you will soon receive a statement showing how much you will receive each month, based on your retirement age. If you are an American, you can contact the Social Security office at www.ssa.gov.

However, If you're forty or younger, there is little chance that Social Security will fully support you in retirement. Because instead of taking away income. You invest that money, pay a small administrative fee, and then pay the returns on the investment; as you would expect a union government to do, this system works differently. Your income is no longer available: what you paid ten years ago was used to pay benefits to other people ten years ago; what you paid last week was used to pay other people last week. And that worked well when the largest generation in American history (the baby boomers) were working, but as they near retirement, the government will probably not be able to collect enough in Social Security income to offset the benefits being paid to boomers. If you are 40 or younger, don't rely on Social Security as part of your retirement package. The money may not be available when it is time to withdraw the income you have deposited. If you do end up getting the benefit, it would be a bonus! As a result, the government has taken two steps: Raise the age for Social Security benefits, And I encourage you to put a lot of money into your retirement accounts that you will use when you retire. The following sections give you examples of how they hope to encourage you to do so.

As you research all of your options, keep track of what is available to you and how much you can legally contribute.

➢ Allow Your Employer to Help You

For most of the 20th century, companies had paid their retirement benefits to their long-term employees, so the employees didn't have to worry about saving for their retirement years how times have changed in the 21st century! Most employees do not stay with companies long enough to be considered long-term, and most companies do not provide any of their own money to support retirement accounts. However, there are some exceptions, which are discussed in the following sections.

Pension plan

Your company deposits money into your retirement account (the amount contributed on your behalf depends on your salary, age, and years of service), manages that account, and pays you benefits from that account when you retire. When you receive an allowance from a pension plan (either monthly, annually, or in a lump sum), your income is taxed.

Profit sharing / 401 (k) / 403 (b) / 457

In this type of plan, your business contributes financially, tax-free, to each account on your behalf based on the amount you request to contribute (the IRS sets limits, but they are too detailed to include here). Some companies match all or part of these donations, making their annual contribution very high. Retirement delivery is taxable. (K) plans used for for-profit businesses; (B) the plans apply to religious, educational, and charitable organizations; 457 plans are used for public and local government employees.

SIMPLE-IRA

A Savings Incentive Match Plan for Employees (SIMPLE) IRA is similar to the traditional IRA and the SEP-IRA. SIMPLE-IRA is established by a company with fewer than 100 employees (including yours if you have a small business). The contribution threshold for the SIMPLE-IRA is currently over $10,000 and is increasing each year.

The employer then commits a portion of his contribution, usually a dollar-for-dollar match, up to 3 percent of his income.

Use any employer-related plan, as the employer offers free retirement benefits. If you can contribute to only one type of retirement account and you have a plan to match your employer with your company, participate in it to the limit!

Employee stock ownership plan

The Employee Stock Ownership Plan (ESOP) is a retirement account made up mainly of company shares paid by your employer and, potentially, You added to the shares of the company you are making. ESOPs can be difficult to take with you when you leave the company, but they are often transferred to the company's stock or cash.

Keep in mind that your ESOP is worth only what your company's stock is worth. If you have any doubts about whether your business will continue to function when you retire, do not count your ESOP income as retirement income.

➢ Invest In Yourself

Besides saving for retirement on defined or sponsored tax plans, you can continuously save and invest in yourself. Remember, however, that you should first take advantage of any free money your employer might be offering in retirement-matching plans, then take advantage of tax-deferred retirement plans, and only as a third choice begin a simple savings account or a more complex investment portfolio for your retirement income.

Investing, which is significantly more complicated, requires specific knowledge of markets, company documents, and business rules. If you are interested in learning more about investing, please do so. If you save on your investment and take the time to read all the available financial documents about the companies you are investing in, the risk is much lower than people think. If you are not interested in doing this, hire a broker or financial advisor to invest your money for you.

Chapter 11: Investing in Stock Market

The stock market is a deep field with many moving averages equal to the market share. The market comprises similar investors, analysts, and media about a company's strengths. The company's strength lies in its ability to show that it is driven by results and ready to grow in the long run.

Stocks with unreliable results or undetectable growth signals have no market share and may fall, stabilize, or overgrow any catalyst. A catalyst can be a news alert, any prominent media coverage, viral event, or celebrity opinion, and lastly, a downgrade or upgrade review of a company by analysts.

The stock market solely depends on each of these data to make the stock exchange work. The public eye watches and responds to these daily events. A strong company will not easily be affected by these events, but it can and will always fall in a particular direction over time.

Technical analysis is a way to determine which direction the stock will go and is widely used in day and swing trading. The most substantial factor is the news and quarterly salary reports. While this strategy is perilous, other approaches are less risky and more useful for long-term trading. Instead of evaluating a company's stock daily, you could consider it on a monthly, quarterly, or annual basis. This is a turnaround strategy for traders. Another proven method is to evaluate a stock for a period of 3 to 5 years. This is an excellent long-term style, and with testing techniques, this can be very useful, mainly when business change is growing and moving towards new ways of doing things. Good examples of this are A.I. (Artificial Intelligence), the legalization of marijuana, streaming-based companies, etc.

➢ Day Trading

As the name implies, day trading means trading, buying, and selling, stocks in one day of trading. Trading positions are invariably closed before the market closes on the day of trading. It is different from after-hours trading, where trading continues even after trading hours every time the stock market closes.

People who buy and sell or participate in intraday trading are called day traders. Although day trading produces a rough trading image during the trading day, this may not be the case when done. You can do a lot of trading, say a dozen, at the time of trading, or you can limit yourself to just one trade.

Sometimes, you can buy a stock one day and sell it the next day if you think selling it the same day will not help. There is no legal restriction that you must terminate your business on the same day. For the most part, you can pay for the trade spread (refer to the difference between two prices, rates, or yields) if you take your trade to the next day. Typically, traders close their trading positions at the end of one trading day. In any case, your trading time depends entirely on your trading strategy for the day or your trading style and practice.

➢ Benefits and risks in day trading

Day traders make quick money and quick losses within minutes or at the end of the trading day. Day trading can evoke the imagination of players playing in gambling establishments. However, there is a marked difference between day trading and gambling.

Technical analysis is something you should learn to understand the technology of knowing when and how to sell by looking at chart patterns. You want to be around people who make this art every day. You want to familiarize yourself with the signs that indicate a change in the stock price. There are various forums and books you can read to find out about this.

While you can't make any of the calculated moves or develop strategies in gambling unless you want to cheat others, day trading involves a deeper understanding of the trading process. You learn about general marketing strategies and stock options. Do some fundamental and technical analysis and stay up to date with the latest news about the stock of the companies you are trading with and much more.

Day trading is not a blind game or just an excellent move. You will have to be careful and cautious before everything else. Therefore, it would be wrong to call day traders a gambler or a robber. Experienced and enthusiastic traders generate a large percentage of profits in day trading. Some retailers can invest millions per year only in day trading. A large number of people especially do day trading to earn money.

However, this does not negate the risk of significant losses in day trading. Those who trade without a calculated strategy and training are more likely to lose day trading significantly. This is especially true of those who borrow money, an act known as buying on margins. They will have to repay the loan with interest and other penalties if they do not profit. This is why day trading is so risky.

➢ Swing Trading

Swing trading is the next level of trading to day trading. Swing trading depends on technical analysis, but only for a more extended period than day trading. Swing trading lasts more than one day but lasts less than three months.

The simple definition of swing trading is that users want to leverage resources by holding a financial instrument overnight to several weeks. As the training guidelines highlight, the goal is to invest in exchange for more significant value than is possible in day trading. You must calculate the position size to minimize risk because you follow a series of high prices and changes.

To do this, people ask for technical analysis to identify low-cost instruments. This means following basic principles and pricing principles and trends.

People seem to do more swing trading than large institutions. This is because large companies are frequently operating heavily to get in and out of security quickly. However, individual traders can make money from short-term changes.

➢ The good side of swing trading

There are several benefits of swing trading, most of which you will find in forums and blogs. These benefits include:

☐ Application: You can apply swing trading to a wide range of markets and instruments. For example, you can predict coins, such as Litecoin (LTC), the big man, Bitcoin (BTC), Ethereum (ETH). Or, you can go with swing trading with standard options.

☐ Resources: many resources on the Internet will help you become a success story. There are e-books, video training courses, PDF files, apps, tutorials, and websites that can give your ideas on stock trading strategies, general trading strategies, and the best tips for spotting patterns. Also, join a Discord discussion to participate in an active trade group.

☐ Tools: You can earn trades using candlesticks charts and other options on various platforms, from Robinhood to MetaTrader. There is the option of using automated bots and expert advisor (EA) Software. Used correctly, this can allow you to make more swing trades than ever.

☐ Mindset: As success stories show, if you have the qualities needed for day trading, you can have the necessary traits for swing trading. For example, are you patient? Do you mind having immense stop losses? Are you happy with taking on a few trades while dealing with the few setups you do? If so, you may already have the skills and training of a successful trader.

➤ The Right Market

Swing trading can be challenging, especially in the two extreme markets - the bear or the bull market. Here you will also find that active stocks will not show the same up-and-down swings as indices that can be stable for weeks.

Instead, you will find in a bear or bull market that momentum always carries stock for a specified period in one defined direction. This can guarantee the best entry point and level-based plan in the long term.

Ideally, it is when the markets are not moving where you have the right place to trade. For example, if you sell on Nasdaq, you will want the index to go up for a few days, down for a few days, and then repeat the pattern. So even though a few months later, your stocks may be in their infancy, you still have plenty of opportunities to make money from short-term changes.

➤ Long Term Investing

A long-term investment is when you hold an asset for more than six months. For example, if you buy 100 shares on Google and then sell them 14 months later, you can get a more prolonged investment. If it's been five years and you still have claims in

Google, it's still a long-term investment. If you choose to sell shares three months or two weeks later, it is a short-term investment.

The reason for the long-term definition of six months or more is mainly tax purposes. In the case of stock, if you hold the stock for a long time, or more than six months, you pay a different tax on capital gains.

One of the biggest challenges facing new investors is that you can't expect to be rich overnight. Deciding to invest wisely is a serious decision, and it will surely help you in the future. But for many people, investing is something that is considered a quick fix. If you want to succeed and grow your money, you can't have that kind of mindset. Instead, you will need to work on achieving some long-term budget. Patience is the key here, and you will need to put forth a long effort if you want to see your money grow.

➢ Principles of Diversity

The first thing to consider when developing your long-term plan is the risk you are willing to take. It is human nature to take a risk, but some people are more willing to than others. It takes time to examine yourself to see the answer to this vital question. For the most part, a long-term investment strategy will include a large base of securities, some potential stocks, and a few more that are a little bit volatile. If you are trying to grow your money for a long time, it is better to go with those blue-chip stocks of well-known trading companies. These companies may not double in a year, but they will provide you with solid growth each quarter.

➤ Be patient with your plan.

If you always have a solid long-term budget, you will need to understand a few things about the market. The truth is, it will go up and down. Things will change over time, and there is nothing you can do about it. You can't be stressed every time your solid stock has a hard day. With a long-term budget, you can see that money grows over a few years. If you have done your homework and have chosen stock with a definite name for growth, don't worry. Markets will change, and your shares will eventually come to life. If you pull the trigger too fast, you could waste your time and capital.

➤ Setting Short-Term and Long-Term Goals

One of the most important rules to keep in mind when making a long-term investment plan is your goals. It isn't easy to work with this type of strategy unless you put everything on paper and follow it through each article. How much money will you invest each month? What is your end goal? How long do you plan to leave your market? By considering these factors, you will make more informed decisions about which actions you prefer. In the same way, you will commit to the plan because you understand the situation in the long term.

Long-term investments are the most common and can be made by that person or provided by the financial institution. A financial institution could be your local banking service or a business company like Charles Schwab, Fidelity, or Edward Jones. If you invest individually in your portfolio of stocks, you will buy each stock based on your research or guidelines.

Most people want to be guided by professional marketing experts daily. Motley Fool is an intelligent and efficient team of analysts. A firm like this would charge for its services or advice. Whether you are investing or receiving a service from a commercial plant, you must monitor your investment regularly. As mentioned, prior, long-term investments can span months or years.

Keep in mind that a brokerage firm will invest your money based on the risk tolerance associated with your investment period or your age. If you are young, then you have time to recover from a risky investment. This is what is called an aggressive investment. Therefore, a young investor has a higher risk tolerance than someone older.

When you reach 30 years old, you will fall into a moderate investor category depending on your tolerance. This is a happy medium between an aggressive investor and a conservative investor. A conservative investor is low risk, is ideal for someone middle-aged or a senior, and is stable, and does not involve any high or moderate risk investments.

➢ Taking Profit

One of the best ways is to learn how to sell investments as an expert. It is easy to buy an investment but getting out separates the amateurs from the pros!

Those who try to stay below or above the value will lose for a long time. Only investors who buy or sell in the middle will ultimately end up moving forward.

Taking profits is when you see what you have achieved and take the initiative to take advantage of it positively or totally. If the stock is performing well, it is a good idea to stay in that stock and sell only part of your position or make a profit. Those profits can be used to reproduce other new positions or however you see fit.

Here are four steps you can take now:

☐ Examine your allocation: Determine what your stock and bond allocation look like now and what it should look like when looking at your goals, then make any necessary changes: The key to determining your stake is when you plan to spend your money.

Think about it for a moment. If we experienced another 2008 market, and stocks fell 50%, how worried would you be? Your stocks bucket three would have 10 years to recover and provide you a decent return before you'd need them to cover your expenses. I hope this gives you added peace of mind knowing that your stock will not be needed for ten years.

THINK LIKE A MILLIONAIRE

Trim down over-concentrated positions: Start thinking like a portfolio manager by setting limits on how much a particular stock will own out of your total portfolio. I would recommend that you do not exceed 10% of your portfolio in any stock before age 55 and not more than 5% in stock after 55 years. The closer you get to retirement, the more you want to be different.

Diversify: I recommend investing your stock portfolio in 8 to 10 stock asset classes, medium, small, overseas assets, growth, value, etc., and three to four bond asset classes using no-load, no-transaction-fee mutual funds or low-cost exchange-traded index funds.

Make your plan and stay on course: Know what to expect from your new portfolio. Hopefully, if you know what to expect, you will not be disappointed when the solution finally comes.

Reinvesting in the right investment is the best option. If you do not make a profit when you should, you lose the opportunity to reinvest in the money you earn. Ideally, you will no longer be investing your first investment, but the money you earn from stocks will increase in value. This is very important in the long run. You are trimming your profits off the top and reinvesting them when appropriate.

Chapter 12: Real Estate Investment

Real estate is defined as immovable property and anything permanently affixed to the property, such as buildings. Investing is the act of using money to buy property to maintain or lease to generate income. It is safe to say then (combining the two definitions) that real estate investing involves purchasing a home (or investments in real estate agencies) to make a profit and acquire wealth.

Unlike investing in stocks (which always seeks more equity for the investor), it is possible to increase investment in real estate (slightly). With real estate investing, you can use other people's money to increase your rate of return and manage a more considerable investment.

However, realtor investing is not a bed of roses. Investing in real estate requires capital, there is a risk, and rental property can be management intensive.

➤ Types of Real Estate Investments

There are many types of real estate investments, and it is crucial to understand what kind of investment and what benefits and risks are involved.

The types of real estate investments we have included the following:

- Real Estate Investment Trusts: These are companies that sell, buy, manage and develop land and properties. These REITs are set up as security traded on all major exchanges, such as stocks, and are invested directly in real estate or real estate agents. These trustees receive special attention in terms of taxes, and they always provide higher returns and are more liquid than other types of investments. People can invest in this type of real estate investment by buying shares directly from the open sale or investment broker.

- Real Estate Partnerships - This is when multiple people combine their money and resources for a single investment purpose. The investment is made through a joint venture with other partners of the real estate investment group.

- Rental Property Leasing - This is a type of real estate investment that provides long-term rental income. This type is considered a long-term investment, but the most massive benefit is that you can sell the property and get the property's value no matter how many years you've been collecting rent on the property. The downside is that, as a landlord, you are responsible for the damage, repair, and maintenance, even if the tenant caused the problem. If a tenant causes the problem, the court has other options available to cover the costs of repairs. This investment property is rented for the short term, and there may be periods when no rental income will arise.

Rental property can be one of the main types of real estate investments in long-term income. This type of investment property generally provides a monthly income unless the property is vacant.

No matter how long you own the investment property, it would be best if you got back at least the value of your original investment, and in most cases, much more. Collect rent as long as you own the property unless your investment does not lose value, then a monthly income minus expenses is a lot like a very high payment. Raw land real estate investment is when a person or company invests in raw land and then profits from the land's natural resources or develops the property.

➢ Getting Acquainted with Real Estate Investment

Suppose you watch cable or satellite television on the weekends. In that case, you can find 20 to 30 channels early in the day by the wealthy retailers that sell everything from books, tapes, seminars, and personal training services. The main focus is on real estate, and they are not worth the time it takes to telephone.

Education plays an essential role in the success of a real estate investor and business knowledge, attitude, and sometimes luck!

Here are some specific steps an investor can take to improve their chances of success.

- ☐ Know the basic concepts of real estate.

As with any investment or business plan, real estate investing has its jargon. There are words and phrases that most of us have never heard before, but we may not know what they mean.

It is important from the beginning to do your research and learn the basics, such as the meanings of words and phrases used in the real estate business daily.

You can start by using the search engine and search for the phrase "descriptions of real estate."

- Start school education.

Home reading has some great benefits. I'm not talking about the lessons we skip over cable T.V. on the weekends; experienced writers recently write many articles in your local library in the real estate investment sector. Look at all the topics you can read during the week and start reading. Write sentences and headings that will appear in books that you are interested in and valuable for your reasoning by investing in real estate. It will be the beginning of your start-up plan.

- Make a game plan.

In the meantime, you have an idea of the general terminology and phrases of the real estate investment world. You have begun to increase your interest and understanding of specific investment strategies. It's time for you to develop your plan and start taking legal action.

Before you can start investing, you need to have a plan for where you are going and how you will get there.

☐   Join local investment organizations.

In each city, state, and government, many organizations assist homeowners. Each of these meetings holds monthly meetings, and some of the best meetings are held weekly, where investors can communicate and learn.

These meetings are important for the first investor because they provide an opportunity to build your team of experienced members. They are also great groups for advice, strategy, and education. Join a group near you and make your presence compulsory. Attend as many meetings as possible each month.

From time to time, the simple act of circulating with like-minded people who are positive and strengthening your determination to succeed may be the most important factor in your future success.

☐   -Find partners, and don't be fooled into getting rich quickly!

One easy mistake to make at first is to go down the "go-alone" path. I also believe that in the corner is a pot of gold that I can get a deal like these guys on T.V.! The only thing rarely said is that most real estate agents have used the past wisely if they are not using it now. Collaboration is a great way to spread investment risk while you learn to manage it. Those risks include spending less money, credit, and time. The partnership can be built into a simple 50/50 one that separates all costs and benefits or more complex alliances. One partner provides funding, and the other providing contracts, tracking, and investment management. Either way, doing it alone can be frustrating, time-consuming, and costly to start investing.

Don't give up your day job!

It's a big mistake that real estate investors sometimes make. Investing in real estate requires a total commitment to the "burning ships" idea. There is no going back when you decide to do your best. And in this report, there is a problem with leaving your first job first.

Take the time to develop your team, make mistakes, generate financial resources, and learn to drive.

These last two pieces of advice go to the heart of why some investors fail but fail miserably. You can most of the time get over mistakes with the first few tips here with patience and a little luck. If you make one of these two mistakes, they can quickly ruin a new investor and ruin a long-term experience.

If you follow all of the tips above, you are more likely to have a team around you to walk you through the two leads and make a hassle-free investment.

Once it has started, DO NOT MAKE A REPAIR.

When estimating investment property repairs, unless you have an experienced contractor and a trusted advisor for your team, you can miss out on a bad sign.

Even the best homeschooling courses may not give you the ability to calculate the cost. It takes experience and time before you can accurately estimate repair costs. Launching an estimated solution can quickly break a bank account and drive profit ownership into the money hole fast!

- Don't buy investment properties in stocks or value.

There is no big mistake that an investor can make today when buying a property by buying it or valuing it in the future. Today's long-term investments focus on real estate and guaranteed monthly cash flow.

Most people who will buy their first investment property in 2019 will view their purchases as a strict investment, and others will consider housing and land to provide new employment. Either way, new investors need to seek all the help, advice, and experience they can get from other investors.

➢ Seeking Cash Buyers for Real Estate

Finding buyers for money is key to the success of the real estate business. Many people get into this business and give up because they know how to get customers. You may have 20 houses to sell, but if you don't have buyers bringing money to the table, you won't sell anything.

Here are some proven ways to attract customers:

    Check with the Local Housing Authority

Trusted sales

Heavy financial institutions

Use the Internet

You can go to public auctions and chat with people who buy properties. It is better to have your business card and write their names and emails to send property to them.

These are just a few of the shared goal-setting programs that you can use. It will help if you need them to get out there and see them.

➤ Finding Motivated Sellers

If you are a real estate agent or think you are one of them, you know (or will know sooner) that real estate investment is about getting big deals, starting with promising sellers.

Here are some ways in which you can do this:

Websites. You can and should have a home shopping website—advertisements in newspapers. You can run newspaper ads of different sizes in different types of advertising to find inspiring marketers. You can place your daily, weekly, monthly, free, and paid news outlets. You can run customized ads or display ads. You can write a copy for direct, non-critical, or commercial editing.

Signs and billboards. Many investors well use garden signs. Some businesses make good use of billboards, bus benches, signals, and other forms of advertising to find sellers who encourage them to buy homes.

Car Advertising. Some investors raise questions and buy houses on posters in their cars and trucks as they walk around town. Some investors purchase ads on buses and other vehicles selling the market.

Yellow Pages. Many investors find that selling in a phone book and especially on yellow pages is an excellent way to generate calls from promotional sellers.

Pay Per Click Advertising. Investors can purchase ads from search engines and online marketing companies to generate traffic on their websites. This may raise questions from the promoters of your real estate agent.

Door to Door Marketing. Some self-employed sellers have gone from house to house buying houses. Or you could use brochures; Post notes, or door hangings to place door-to-door sales to make calls.

Selected Advertising websites. Websites such as Craigslist, Backpage, and other free or low-cost marketing websites help generate queries for promotional marketers.

Direct email. Sending a list of multiple owners' items can effectively generate calls to promotional vendors - postcards, letters, etc., and mailing lists for absent homeowners, filed notices, vacant homes, etc.

➢ Finding Lenders to Fund Your Deals

To start making money with property, you will need to learn where and how to get the money. As a real estate agent, you can have plans instead of going to the bank to buy the property. You can take out a mortgage or a complete home for a profit. You can also pay with cash. Once you have acquired a lot and managed to put it under contract, continue to fund your grant.

If you find a perfect property and need to provide immediate funding, you will need to find a lender to finance your contract. You can use creditors such as Visio Borrowing, Borrowing, Real Transaction Cost, etc.

➢ Sealing Your First Deal

Once you have completed that initial agreement, you will know what to expect and find that it is not as difficult as you thought.

You will learn about what you did well and what adjustments you need to make for next time. Take this experience and try to analyze what made it work so well. Apply it to your next contract.

The following real estate investment opportunity should be more relaxed and come more naturally to you with careful consideration. Every transaction is different from the last one, but this is what makes this business fun. You will need to design and keep learning and growing your business.

Chapter 13: Investing in Cryptocurrency

If you've been following the news, you've probably heard of the term "cryptocurrency." You must have heard that they can increase in value rapidly, or their prices sometimes alter overnight, never to return. Have you ever wondered if you should invest in them?

Then let's dive in.

If you invest in this new area, it is up to you to do a little research and see what makes a new investment a different or unique alternative. Your research will determine how much you believe in the future of your savings for such a new ad. There's an almost unanimous consensus about the potential of the blockchain. Some say that the blockchain is the most important thing since the start of the Internet. Billions of dollars have been invested. Where cryptocurrencies are the same in the future, where the blockchain remains the same, will determine whether these currencies can pay a large amount of money in your investment portfolio. Nobody wants to miss out should cryptocurrency start paying off.

Investing in bitcoins or another cryptocurrency is like any other type of investment: the more you know, the better your strategy, and the more intelligent it is. And there are many opportunities to pay.

➢ **What are Cryptocurrencies?**

At its most basic level, cryptocurrencies are a straightforward situation. They are digital currencies made online and designed to spend money on the Internet. Developed with software code, cryptocurrencies are a way to transfer value, often digitally, like when you buy something online. The first and most popular currency is Bitcoin.

Some bitcoins are the same as a quarter, except they are unstoppable. It's a piece of code, and only you, as the owner, have the I.D., known as the coin key. You can transfer another I.D. to someone else so that they can buy something. Then that person gets a new bitcoin key, and the old I.D. has expired. You cannot hold bitcoins. You cannot hear. But when a person accepts bitcoin, he sees it in the same way as a quarter.

Bitcoins have become more expensive because the entire community has grown up around the cryptocurrency craze, determined to give bitcoin owners more and more in that currency.

➢ **Getting Ahead**

Now that you understand why you want to invest and the risks involved, the next step is to buy coins. But it is unlike any other investment you have ever made. Remember, this is not the same as exchanging U.S. dollars for euros at an airport while on vacation in Europe. Because the cryptocurrency investment is made on the Internet, you cannot hold your purchases (unless you splurge for a gold bitcoin offered by certain retailers). Instead, it is in the code developed wind, which creates problems in maintaining and protecting your investment. It will require you to go through unusual obstacles to sell your investment. It is not like going to your local bank.

➤ Choosing an Exchange platform

When you decide that it is time to invest, you will have to opt for an exchange platform. You will want to evaluate which one works best for your region and which payment method works best for you. While many exchanges have come and gone, here are a few names that remain prominent in the U.S. and elsewhere:

Coinbase (United States)

Coincheck (Japan)

Bitstamp (Luxembourg)

CEX.IO (London)

Coinplug (South Korea)

Korbit (South Korea)

Kraken (United States)

When you make a purchase, say $50, after which the exchange will take a portion of the money as fees to continue the transaction. Some of the funds will support the change itself. If miners have to proceed with a transaction, part of the fee goes towards paying the transaction fee on the blockchain that resides in their cryptocurrencies. While you can easily find exchanges with fees of around 0.1 percent, it's important to remember that some tokens are priced higher to buy internally. That can increase costs, especially if it's a more complex coin to make and validate.

➤ How many cryptos Should You Buy?

The amount you spend will determine the number of fees you pay, as they are always a percentage of the total amount you want to buy. However, most exchanges will reduce the cost they wish to continue with the payment if you spend a considerable amount. By purchasing only, a small amount, you will be subjected to high fees.

Depending on how much you plan to invest, wait a few days before buying or selling your coins. Part of this time has to do with money itself; it is quick to buy Ripple's XRP as no miner needs to confirm the purchase. This leads to faster repair times. On the other hand, Bitcoin is always moving slowly, as the public has to assure you while you can set a monetary value at the time of purchase, that means you can't sell for a few days. If the coin is suddenly three times over three hours after your purchase, you cannot sell right away. You will have to wait a few days to a week before the coins arrive in your digital wallet. At that point, who knows? Your bitcoin reward may disappear.

The waiting time will depend on how much you buy. Buy a large amount, and you can get it in a few days (or minutes, depending on the exchange). So, it's just a question of whether there is enough supply to support the current purchase. For senior users, there is no guarantee that your purchase will be sufficient in the market when you start making a payment as determined by the amount of money being sold.

➢ Top Coins to Invest In

Bitcoin (BTC): When you start investing in cryptocurrencies, you will doubtless have a share of your investments in bitcoins. That's the best word in the post, and avoiding bitcoin is like not investing in Apple within your stock portfolio. It is not wise to avoid it altogether unless you want to bet against the current market trend. With that being said, you still don't understand why it could be such a great coin, and even worse, even if it could continue to be a staple in cryptocurrencies. Ethereum (ETH): Ethereum has become the most popular and well-known name in the long list of altcoins and is just behind bitcoin in terms of its trading volume. However, unlike bitcoin, Ethereum has two sides. There is a start-up company that is building a business about blockchain technology. There is also ether, a symbol used to do business within the Ethereum network and the money you buy when you buy a name.

Ripple (XRP): Unlike ether and ether, the Ripple blockchain is built with controls that allow the company to determine the time and money to be distributed to the public. It made a distinctive mark inside the coin from this control until the crypto community enforced the change. Critics have compared it to the Federal Reserve, which regulates funding. Despite attempts to contain criticism, this Ripple XRP extinguishes many crypto lovers who believe these coins should work outside the company. Meanwhile, some see the technology and strategy as an innovation, supported by the growth of customers approaching Ripple to participate in the blockchain.

Stellar (XLM): It is not surprising that the signal generated in the Ripple protocol had an unusual setting, and so does Stellar and its signal, Lumens (XLM). In 2014, Stellar.org was created to bring the bank's power to the world's most vulnerable areas. Because it remains incapable of having the economy of big companies to work in areas with significant poverty, residents are ignored. But they need the power to send and receive money, sometimes from other countries, to run a business or other common necessity. Stellar wants to bring the ability to make things easier in these parts of the world.

Litecoin (LTC): When Bitcoin arrived on the scene, developers and engineers immersed in the digital currency community were quick to jump on the bandwagon, looking for ways to improve and enhance content. But the bitcoin code is open source, which means that anyone can crib much of the program with a few tweaks and then increase their revenue stream. These coins from the bitcoin code are numerous, but there is one in particular that has seen an increase in its value over the years. Charlie Lee produced Litecoin in October 2011. He took the bitcoin code, changed the location inside the code he thought held bitcoin, then pulled it out of the field, attracting users and investors. We appeal because of the Litecoin-offered set and Lee's loyalty to the table as a coin cheerleader.

Cardano (ADA): When research firm Weiss Ratings developed its list of secure crypto names, an unknown start in the space, Cardano earned one of the highest marks in technology and adoption perspective. This is a new coin, released only in October 2017, but based on Weiss's rating, it is clear that it already has a significant interest. Despite its status as a very young name in cryptocurrencies, it has become a reality among the top ten currencies based on commercial capital. What drove this coin into the top echelon of crypto options? Cardano, which has a crypto name under the name ADA, has developed new content and design, pushing it forward in the eyes of blockchain lovers.

NEO: China is known for being an unfriendly place for cash inflows. In the years that bitcoin has grown into a stable name in space, China has done a lot to reduce the excitement around fashion, at least within its nation. That is why it is strange that the Shanghai-based cryptocurrency has become one of the most popular cryptocurrency markets. This is because NEO can achieve something that few cryptocurrencies have a chance to do: it could be Chinese crypto.

NEM-Similar to Cardano, NEM provides a change in the way things are done and new collections. While bitcoin uses the content of proof of work in its blockchain, which provides a way for miners to continue transactions, Cardano uses the proof of stake, rewarding those who have more coins to dictate how to make the transaction of importance. This is an adjustment that has made NEM altcoin growing among fans. It is becoming a growing blockchain phenomenon in Japan.

Regularly evaluate your investment ideas.

When you start researching cryptocurrency terms and get into this thing that separates one from the other, no doubt, you will begin to make comments and speculations about each other. Some you will begin to embrace, be happy, and support. Others you will doubt, turn your back on them, or call them frauds. This will form the basis of your initial investment and sign a growing understanding of the crypto environment.

Remember, though, that you will have to revisit these ideas as time goes on. At first, you may believe that financial institutions will never use XRP in their daily activities. But after six months, if more companies register, you will have to re-evaluate that idea. You can believe that ether will surpass bitcoin as the preferred currency among leading crypto users. But if the ether has lost track of bitcoin after a year, you will have to go back to that original discourse and decide whether to hold on to the mind or change your mind. As you do so, you can change the shape of your portfolio to reflect your ideas.

Also, since this is not about the money you trust, it is better to have a mental attitude and accept research and results. This is the only way you will feel like you have anything to do with the game without wasting some dollars.

Chapter 14: Investing Tips From the World's Successful Investors

Investors may disagree a lot, but one thing they agree, that making money from the market comes with a solid strategy based on a specific set of rules. Think for a moment about your first few days as an investor. If you are like many others, you have jumped at the very edge of the market. When you made a purchase, I bet you didn't understand what bid-ask spread was, and you sold very early if the stock was up or too late if the stock had fallen.

If you do not have a well-designed set of investment rules, now is the time to do so, and the best place to start is to learn from successful investors and how they handled or are handling their investment business. Not only do we find people who can claim success, but they are also some of the most successful investors in history.

All successful investors have one thing in common: they have rules.

Do Research

Warren Buffett is considered to be the most successful investor in history. Not only is he one of the richest men in the world, but he also has the financial support of many presidents and world leaders. When Buffett speaks, the world markets go by his words.

"It's better to buy a good company at a good price than a good company at an amazing price."

Buffett is known for being a successful teacher. His annual letter to his company's investors, Berkshire Hathaway, is used in college finance classes at most prestigious universities.

Buffett offers two key tips when evaluating a company: First, look at the company's quality and then the price. Observing the company's quality requires you to read the financial statements. It is only after gaining confidence in the quality of the company that the price will be tested.

If the company is not a quality company, do not buy it because the price is low.

Be Convinced

Bill Gross is the co-founder of PIMCO. He was in charge of the PIMCO Total Return Fund, one of the largest funds in the world, and was the chief investment officer of the company before he left in 2014.

The overall policy focuses on portfolio management.

"Do you like a certain stock? Put about 10% of your portfolio in it. Make the impression calculated. A good idea [of investment] should not be divided into irrational forgetfulness."

The universal principle is one that most small investors know differently - that is, do not put all your investments in one name.

Dividing is a good rule of thumb; it can lower your reward if one of your choices makes a big move while other words don't.

Investing in a market also means taking risks based on thorough research. Always keep cash in your account for opportunities that require less money, and do not be afraid to do so if you think your research articles have been successful.

Have an Investment Philosophy

"Opportunities abound. When it rains gold, put out the bucket, not the thimble," were the wise words of one of today's investors, Warren Buffet.

Warren Buffett's investment philosophy has always been based on a firm decision. Understand the business and if you see it as relevant, bet more on it. Many novice investors try to impersonate him, and therefore, they lose money.

People who do not have an investment philosophy to guide them can follow fashion trends and unstable trends for a long time.

Carl Icahn is an investor who fights for money and marketing attacks today, buying big stakes from companies and trying to get voting rights to increase shareholder value. Some of its properties include Time Warner, Yahoo, Clorox, and Video Blockbuster. One of the most important rules of Icahn is that when you invest, you must not take anything personally. Icahn has obtained his fair share of enemies over the years, but investors should not strictly follow his advice about interpersonal relationships. "How many times in your past savings have you read an article, watched a news report, or received advice from a trusted friend about hot stock and financial loss?"

There is only one tip you can do: Use your in-depth research based on facts (not opinions) obtained from reliable sources. Some tips can be considered and validated, but they should not be the only reason to commit to making money.

Take a Long-Term View

Buffett also suggests that stocks be a long-term investment, ignoring the economic and political situation that could lead to short-term stock prices. Buffett is always looking at stocks becoming part of the business, so he is always looking at the potential for profit from these businesses over the next five years or more.

Let the Winners Run

Dennis Gartman began publishing the Gartman Letter in 1987. Daily information about the world trade markets sent to hedge funds, brokers, mutual funds, and industry worldwide each morning. Gartman is also a successful businessman and regularly visits the financial network.

"Be patient with business success; don't be too impatient with job losses. Remember that it is possible to make a lot of sales/investments if we are 'right' only 30% of the time if our losses are small and our profits are big."

His previous rule deals with the mistakes made by small investors. First, do not sell at the first sign of profit; let successful activities continue. Second, don't miss out on lost sales. Investors who make money in the market agree to lose a small amount of money in the trade, but they do not want to lose a lot of money.

As Gartman points out, you do not have to be perfect for a long time. Most importantly, implement a successful trade and get out of the lost trade as soon as possible. If you follow this rule, the money you make from successful marketing will be much higher than for lost trades.

Try to Avoid Fees

Broker fees can consume your investment return, which is why Buffett is a follower of the most affordable interest rates. Fund Manager Peter Lynch and author of Learn to Earn: A Guide for Beginners in Investment and Business Foundations informs readers of this book about "direct investment programs" in which investors can invest directly in the company and the investor month, without paying commissions. The investor gets to buy more shares every month without paying fees and without a broker. Investors should first find out which company they are eligible to invest in before pursuing this strategy.

Overall, there is a lot to learn from successful investors and their experiences. Each of these investors is known as a market student and leader. As you begin to apply these principles and commit to following them even though your mind may say otherwise, you should do well in marketing.

Look Forward to the Future

One of the richest men in the world, Carlos Slim, owns hundreds of companies and has more than 250,000 employees. Slim points out that it is one of the immense investment opportunities in fighting poverty in Mexico and Latin America. Successful investors are not looking at what is happening right now. Instead, by learning about the company's power or the economy as a whole and how it communicates with its competitors, they are investing now in the future and thinking ahead.

If you are currently looking or trying to jump on an investment bandwagon that has already made a short-term profit, you have certainly missed the big move. Try to find the next big winner, but always stick to your portfolio with big companies with a long history of consistent growth.

Patience is Key.

You may not have heard of Prince Alwaleed Bin Talal, but he is well known in the investment world. An investment from Saudi Arabia, he founded the Kingdom Holding Company. He then made a major bet on Citigroup's predecessor (C) Citicorp in the early 1990s, becoming a significant shareholder in the bank.

Also, he invested in Twitter (TWTR) and SNAPCHAT. His patience was tested during the Great Recession of 2008, when most of his investments were affected.

"I'm a long-termer. I'm not a seller." —Prince Alwaleed Bin Talal

When others sold, especially when Citi was under intense pressure in the late 1990s, Prince Alwaleed Bin Talal did what other good investors were doing to collect his wealth: hold their investment. Investors who have strong faith and do research can hold back for a long time, looking at challenging market events and making good profits.

Motivation Hub: Inspiring Stories of Successful People

The Janitor That Proved You Don't Need A Big Paycheck to Build A $9 Million Fortune

Ronald James Read was an American who worked as a gas station attendant and a security guard. He grew up in Dummerston, Vermont, in a poor home environment. He walked or drove 6.4 kilometers every day to high school and was the first in his family to go to high school. During World War II, he enlisted in the United States military, serving in Italy as a military police officer. Following the honorable discharge from the army in 1945, Read returned to Brattleboro, Vermont, where he worked for a gas station and mechanic for 25 years. He retired for a year and then took a full-time cleaning job at JCPenney, where he worked for 17 years until 1997.

Read lived frugally and enjoyed investing in stocks while studying the market. The Wall Street Journal noted that his purchase of about $ 2,380 for $39 from Pacific Gas and the Electricity Company on January 13, 1959, grew to $10,735 when he died.

Read went to buy more shares of The J.M. Smucker Company, CVS Health, and Johnson & Johnson also held long-term holdings for many blue-chip companies, including Procter and Gamble, JPMorgan Chase, General Electric, and Dow Chemical Company.

THINK LIKE A MILLIONAIRE

He focused on companies that paid generous shares, which he would support to purchase additional shares. He did not invest in technology companies or day trading stock because he was mainly focused on companies he knew.

He had less than 95 different stocks in many industries at the time of his death, such as health care, telecommunications, equipment, train transportation, banks, and consumer goods. Although he had shares in Lehman Brothers when it went bankrupt in 2008, the situation only slightly affected his return because Read diversified his investment.

In a secure deposit box in his bank, Read kept his stock certificates which when reached about five inches high when piled together. To keep up to date on his investment, he relied on the Wall Street Journal, the Barron, and the nearby public library.

When he died at the age of 92 in 2014, Ronald Read left $1.2 million at the local library and $4.8 million in the hospital, where he ate breakfast every day, Always peanut butter English muffin and a cup of coffee.

Although he did not make much money, he invested along the way and closely followed the stock market to get the most out of his portfolio.

Most importantly, Ray knew the value of slow growth and the importance of reinvesting his profits back in his portfolio. He focused on creating wealth and created a satisfying life, independent of flashy cars or fancy living to bring him happiness.

At the time of his death, Read earned $ 8 million in equal investment.

The Secretary That Turned $180 Worth of Abbott Stock Into $7 Million.

In the early 1990s, an American lady named Grace Groner was recognized after her death for a $7 million gift to her alma mater at Lake Forest College. Groner was born in 1909 on a small farm in Lake County, Illinois. She had a twin sister, Gladys, who died in April 2007.

As a 12-year-old orphan, both sisters were adopted by George Anderson, one of the most important members of society. He paid for both of them to go to nearby Lake Forest College, where they graduated in 1931. Grace Groner never married.

For years, Groner lived with an elderly relative of George Anderson, Ann Findlay, in a small building. The Anderson family has always considered her to be "family."

Grace began working as a secretary for Abbott Labs in 1931 and had been with the company for 43 years. Four years later, she bought 3 shares of Abbott for $60 each, totaling an investment of $ 180.

Groner allowed those shares to grow, and in her lifetime, she continued to reinvest her shares. She had few needs, lived in a small country house she had been entrusted with, bought clothes for sale, but she traveled a lot. She also gave money to those in need, but she kept her name secret.

At the time of her death at the age of 100, her original 3 shares had turned into more than 100,000 shares due to stock divisions, dividends, and prices.

And thanks to a professional investment approach, Grace Groner turned $ 180 to $ 7 million over 75 years.

Groner left most of her possessions at her alma mater, at Lake Forest College. This allows 1,300 students to pursue opportunities they may not have had, such as study courses and study programs abroad.

Her foundation has renovated her home. It now houses women at Lake Forest College in their teens who have made significant contributions to the college community and have received a grant in the foundation. The women stayed in the house as Grace's guests - an estimated 1,300 students will benefit from his will. The house will be known as "Grace's Cottage."

Now here's an important lesson you can learn from Grace. According to Spectrum magazine of Lake Forest College, Groner was "particularly restrained" with her money.

She got her clothes at rummage sales and lived in a simple one-room closet. Her items included simple furniture, uneven dishes, and vintage T.V. Instead of having a car, Grace chose to walk.

Although Abbott's shares were divided over the years, Grace did not sell her shares.

The idea of starting small and reinvesting funds over several decades was how she slowly built her multi-million-dollar fortune.

Man Discovers Old Printing Machine in Dirty Barn and Turns it into $25 Million-Dollar Business.

The amazing story of the millionaire begin with a blue man from cooking hamburgers and hot dogs to working at the Coca-Cola delivery port, the assembly line at the factory, waiting for tables in many restaurants, and finally finding his way to become a Million-dollar multi-entrepreneur CEO. In 2005, Dr. Riess graduated from the University of Cincinnati in Marketing/Entrepreneurship. After graduating and moving to Colorado, Dru tested the corporate world for a year but returned to waiting tables at Colorado Springs. Eager to do more in his life, he held his head up and looked for the opportunity to do something special. Maybe Texas might be the place where his dreams would come true.

With no printing experience, no business experience, and not even the availability of resources, Dru leveraged an opportunity everyone has shunned. His friend knew a young man who owned an old broken printing press, and when asked if he would like to rebuild it, his friend gave up on that idea as well.

However, a friend of Riess's told the guy about Riess, and the recruiting process began to bring Dru from Colorado to Texas to start the rebuilding process. In the summer of 2007, Dru took a shot of his life traveling to Texas to resurrect the print press inadvertently.

New to Texas in 20017, Dr. Reiss came across an old printing press in a friend's barn. After finding out about him by Googling, Reiss began to learn about the publishing industry.

Reiss wanted to start using the old printing press that he acquired to learn how the printing industry works because he always wanted to be an entrepreneur. So, he embarked on a long journey to start a business.

In 2008, his friend Roy Salinas joined him as a business partner. The two of them traveled 3,500 miles across the country in a rented purple Chevy, sleeping on friends' floors along the way.

Along the journey, the partners find their publishing business in front of several decision-makers, hoping that someone will give their unfamiliar business a chance.

The company grew rapidly, and eventually, the pair bought it from the original owners.

In 2016, "Popular Ink" made $25 million in annual sales.

"I am convinced that nobody can become a millionaire. You got it, you want it, "Riess said in an interview with CNBC in 2017," If you believe in yourself, you might have a chance to become a millionaire. "

The 96-Year-Old Woman Who Amassed A $9 Million Fortune By Duplicating Her Boss's Investment Strategy Secretly

Sylvia Bloom lived modestly as a secret millionaire. She typically rides the subway to Street Law Firm, where she worked as a secretary. She was responsible for controlling her boss's stock portfolio. Bloom continued working for a law firm for 67 years and died shortly after that in 2016.

Also, she built a fortune that was divided between 3 commercial houses and 11 banks.

Bloom was frugal but not cheap. For example, she was well dressed and hairy. The fur coat she had, however, was a decent Persian lamb and not an expensive ermine.

She amassed her wealth by focusing on investing lawyers in her office, who constantly asked her to return their investment options on the stock market to their brokers. Over the years, she learned the patterns and learned to trust many bets on her great resource. The most interesting thing was that she did not reveal her wealth, and she continued her career-long after collecting millions in shares.

THINK LIKE A MILLIONAIRE

When Sylvia passed away in 2016, she was worth $9 million and left $8.2 million in cash. After her passing, her close friends and family were shocked to learn of Bloom's wealth.

Ms. Bloom spent her life getting her stock back rather than spending a fortune on her investment. Sylvia and her husband, a firefighter, would have lived on Park Avenue but preferred to live in a rented house.

In large part, Sylvia Bloom's story is strange because deferred profits over a lifetime are not easy.

Perhaps her mind was moved by the new company she was working for, and she returned in 1946. The Cleary Gottlieb Steen & Hamilton law firm, where Grace worked for 67 years, became one of the law firms most successful worldwide.

In the 1940s, the firm was small and ambitious; its wealth wasn't confirmed. In the space of 67 years, the Cleary Gottlieb Law Firm has grown to more than 1,200 attorneys. The New York law firm is now known for advising countries struggling to pay off their debts.

As a longest-serving company employee, Ms. Bloom became a trusted tool and grew to nurture many relationships. She got married later, and the theory for many was that even her husband was not fully aware of his wife's fortune because the couple lived in a small rent-controlled house. A stalwart stoic, Ms. Bloom was famous for always walking the subway to and from work, even on

September 11, 2001. On that fateful day, she forcefully walked across the Brooklyn Bridge and took a bus home instead of a taxi.

Her legacy is a legacy of generosity, humility, and philanthropy that deserves its documentary and an almost unbelievable story in this age of technology and visualization.

Dyslexic Kid Starts Record Company in Church Crypt and Becomes 4th Richest Citizen in the U.K.

Innovator and entrepreneur Richard Branson has been called "one of today's most ardent CEOs." Branson expressed his desire to become an entrepreneur at a young age.

At first, things weren't so easy for Branson. In an interview with CNN Money, Mogul explained that "they saw me as the bravest person in school," he said, "it never occurred to me to be successful."

As a child, Branson had dyslexia, which affected his performance in school. His notes suffer, but his love grows. On his last day of school, his principal, Robert Drayson, told him that he would either end up in prison or become a millionaire.

Branson's parents supported his efforts at a young age. His mother was a merchant; One of his most successful endeavors was building and selling wooden meat crates and paper containers. In London, he started with a break from 1967 to 1968.

THINK LIKE A MILLIONAIRE

At age 15, Branson launched a magazine called "The Student" because he "wanted to edit the magazine" and realized that students did not produce national student books.

This Magazine didn't make him money. However, he made a small profit selling mail-order records by email and advertisements in classified magazines.

Soon after, Richard Branson opened his first recording studio, which later turned into a record label.

Virgin Records continued to be one of the best and most popular record-keeping sites of all time.

The record company eventually became Virgin Brand and now employs more than 70,000 people.

Branson has been involved in many failed businesses, such as Virgin Cars, Virgin Cola, Virgin Brides, Virgin Publishing, and Virgin Clothing.

However, Branson has an optimistic perspective of failure. He wrote: "I think the secret of hindsight is not only the threat of failure but also its use as a motivational and learning tool. There is nothing wrong with making mistakes as long as you don't do the same thing repeatedly. new."

Over time, Branson created 12 billion different companies and was named the world's most influential person in 2007. As of 2017, his value is more than $ 5.1 billion.

Branson's first book, Losing My Virginity, tells the story of how he built a student magazine with one of the best tools ever.

His most recent book, a story about his life titled "Finding My Virginity," describes the triumphs and failures of his 50 years as an entrepreneur.

Man Leaves Budapest in 1965 at the age of 21 and Arrives in America Broke. Today, He's Worth $20.3 Billion.

Peterffy was born in Budapest, Hungary, on September 30, 1944, in a basement of a hospital during a Russian airstrike. His father emigrated to the United States after the failure of the 1956 Revolution in Hungary.

Thomas Peterffy, then known as Péterffy Tamás, left his engineering studies in Hungary and moved to the United States to join his father in New York in 1965.

When his father, who was living with his second wife, had no place to live for his son, he gave Thomas $100 and told him to do something for himself. Then began a journey that would transform a penniless refugee into a billionaire.

When she moved to New York City, she did not speak English. Peterffy began his career in the United States as a design draftsman working on road projects at an engineering company. He volunteered to develop a newly purchased computer program at this company, which eventually shaped his future course.

THINK LIKE A MILLIONAIRE

In his background for the program, Peterffy said, "I think the way a CEO runs his company reflects his experience. The business is a collection of programs, and my job is to make those programs as much money as possible.

Peterffy gave up his job designing financial model software and bought a seat on the US Stock Exchange to sell stock options. During his financial career, he was constantly pressured into adopting automated processes rather than manual ones. He wrote the code in his head during the trading day and then applied his ideas to computer trading models hours later.

Peterffy eventually developed computer models for stock trading and transformed the stock trading industry into a portable computer market.

Peterffy created chaos among retailers by bringing hand-held computers to the trading floor in the early 1980s. His business affiliated with his position at AMEX eventually became Interactive Brokers. He resigned as CEO in 2019.

Today, Thomas is the CEO and founder of Interactive Brokers Group, Inc. (I.B.). Interactive Brokers is a company that sells discounts on the Internet in America. The company dates back to 1977 when Peterffy bought a seat on the United States Stock Exchange as a sole trader and made T.P. & Co the next year.

The company has several securities operating in the largest stocks, futures, bonds, currencies, and exchange options worldwide. The company began a public offering on May 4, 2007, under the Nasdaq ticker: IBKR in the Nasdaq exchange.

On October 5, 2018, Interactive Brokers submitted their list to IEX, becoming the primary founder of the exchange. Barron's Magazine reported in 2009 that Interactive Brokers maintain the site as "the cheapest trading platform for investors," and Barron went on to earn a position as a low-cost broker and leading online retailer in 2019.

Today, Peterffy owns 75% of the Interactive Brokers net worth of $19.5 billion in January 2018. Previously, he was the richest man in the United States and the three richest men in Connecticut. That same year, Thomas Peterffy was ranked 22nd in the Forbes 400 annual list of Forbes 400. He was the richest Hungarian in the world in 2019.

Man, Who Grew up Picking Cotton with No Shoes Builds $10 Billion Oil Company.

Harold Hamm had to work in the cotton fields as a child in Oklahoma. At 16, he left home at the age of 17 to find work repairing and pumping gasoline in Enid, Okla, to support the family.

In his junior year of high school, Harold's family moved to Enid, Oklahoma. At the time, Enid was an oil town in the middle of an oil field. Hamm was impressed by the "oil people," whom he described as interested and "greater than life."

When it got to a time for him to write a high school dissertation, Harold wrote his dissertation on petroleum oil. This allowed him to look inside the factory, turn his interest in oil. Shortly after that, he began dreaming of becoming an oil exploration.

After high school, Hamm began working in the oil fields as a truck driver and began learning more about the oil industry. Along the way, he welcomed a group of consultants who taught him about fountains, oil, and geography.

Within a few years, young Harold found a cosigner that helped him get a loan to start his own business, Harold Hamm Trucks. He went on to study business and, at the age of 25, dug his first well.

Harold Hamm's first well was not a huge success, but it paid for itself and gave Hamm the confidence to try another. The second was very lucrative, and he spent the profit on attending college and getting educated.

Hamm's love of oil has boosted his determination to continue learning and exploring new ideas in the industry.

Eventually, Hamm became the founder, president, and CEO of Continental Resources, a $10 billion oil company.

People around him in his hometown of Enid, OK, encouraged Harold to succeed. He noted that a special person, a sculptor who spoke at one of the school conventions, encouraged him.

In an interview with Forbes magazine, Hamm said of the sculptor: "It was clear that he worked well because it was his love, his art, and the message was that we could all do well if we follow our love in life."

From Being A Bartender to Having an Estimated Net Worth of $4.4 Billion

Mark Cuban, the billionaire owner of the Dallas Mavericks football team, cannot be confused with someone who didn't get everything they wanted in life.

But did you know that Cuba started as a garbage bag salesman that relied on food exchanges in his early years?

Cuba was born in Pittsburgh, Pennsylvania. His father, Norton Cuban, was a driver. Cuba has described his mother, Shirley, as someone who "has a different job or different career goals every week." He grew up in the small town of Pittsburgh in Lebanon in a family of Jewish workers.

His paternal grandfather changed his last name from "Chabenisky" to "Cuban" after his family left Russia on Ellis Island. His grandparents, also Jewish, came from Romania.

THINK LIKE A MILLIONAIRE

On July 7, 1982, the Cuban moved to Dallas, Texas, where he first got a job as a bartender on Greenville Avenue in Elan and later as a software provider for his business, one of the first computer providers in the United States. He was laid off less than a year later after meeting with a client to find a new business instead of opening a store.

Even in college, various side jobs helped pay off his bills, but success at a computer consulting business helped him earn his first million. With that, he recreated a web distribution empire that increased his net worth, allowing him to buy a large chunk of Maverick in 2000.

Cuba also helps companies with social Software and network business distribution. He is the owner of Ice Rocket, a search engine that offers a content blog.

Cuba has started his own company, Micro Solutions, with the support of his previous clients in his Software. Micro Solutions was originally an integration process with a software vendor. The company was the first to announce technologies such as Carbon Copy, Lotus Notes, and CompuServe. One of the clients of large companies is Perot Systems.

The company grew to more than $30 million in revenue, and in 1990, Cuban sold Micro Solutions to CompuServe, then backing H&R Block for $ 6 million. He made about $ 2 million after taxes on the transaction.

Cuban was a partner in Red Swoosh, a company that uses peer-to-peer technology to deliver rich media, including video and Software, to a user's P.C., later acquired by Akamai. He was also an investor in Weblogs, Inc., acquired by AOL.

In 2005, Cuban invested in Brondell Inc., the first San Francisco to make a high-rise Swash toilet that acts like a bidet, but it is becoming a standard toilet. "People tend to approach technology in the same way, either in front of them or behind them," Cuban said.

He has invested in Goowy Media Inc., an online software start-up in San Diego. In April 2006, Sirius Satellite Radio announced that Cuban would host his weekly radio show Mark Cuban on Radio Maverick. However, the program did not come to hold.

In July 2006, Cuban sponsored Sharesleuth.com, a website created by an investigative journalist from St. Louis. To test a new business model to make online journalism financially viable, Cuban has announced that he will take over the shares of the companies described on Sharesleuth.com before publication.

Business analysts and lawmakers question the advisability of downsizing the shares before making public statements that could result in a loss in value. Cuban insisted that the act be legal given the full declaration.

In April 2007, Cuban partnered with Mascot Books to publish his first children's book, Let's Go, Mavs! In November 2011, he wrote a 30,000-word e-book, How to Succeed In Business Games: If I

Can Do It, You Can Do It, which he described as "a way to get inspired."

In October 2008, Cuban launched Bailoutsleuth.com as a site, an online site for the U.S. government's "bailout" of $ 700 million for financial institutions.

In September 2010, Cuban offered an undisclosed amount of savings to keep former analytics company Motionloft. According to the company's manager, Jon Mills, he sent a message to Cuban about the business proposition. He said that Cuban responded immediately, stating that he would like to hear more. Mills praised the sentence for founding the company.

In November 2013, several investors questioned Cuban about Mill's representation of the Motionloft acquisition. Cuban denied an acquisition was in place.

Mills was fired as CEO of Motionloft by the owners on December 1, 2013, and in February 2014, he was arrested by the FBI and charged with wire fraud. Mills misrepresented to investors that Motionloft was going to be acquired by Cisco.

Cuban has gone on record to state that the technology, which at least in part is meant to serve the commercial real estate industry, is "game-changing for tenants.

In 2019, Mark Cuban, Steve Watts, his wife Angela, and Ashton Kutcher invested a 50% stake in Veldskoen's fledgling U.S. business.

Today, it's estimated that Cuban is worth about $4.4 billion.

Conclusion

You may feel overwhelmed by all the information presented in this book. Being overwhelmed can be a good thing because even though you feel like all that information is too much for you to absorb, your brain gets to work unconsciously.

By resetting and rejuvenating your mind, you can transform the social mirror that praises mediocrity and chastises a person's success and freedom.

Believe it or not, you can change your life for the better. However, it would help if you did not approach it with the same sense of where you are at the moment. You will need to embrace the love and knowledge to take your mind to the next level. You have to think like a millionaire!

When your business is up and running, the work doesn't stop there. Because this is a business, you have to manage it and regularly work to improve all areas.

No one said that dealing with money would be easy, but it would be interesting and satisfying. Financial planning gives you the tools you need to achieve goals and overcome challenges along the way.

Imagine that a millionaire has already provided you with all the information you will need for the entire trip, including the basics for finding the right mindset, starting a business, saving and investing, etc. The activities in this guide help you get an idea of where you are financially and what you do next.

The investment landscape is complex and involves a commitment to understanding its use. Once you understand its application, you can apply it to your life. The sooner you get involved, the better. You do not have to be perfect to start a project. Once you start, you will learn more from the experience of not watching or reading. However, it needs information to be calculated. Take the steps listed to take the risk that will not affect your healthy lifestyle. The better you get, the more you can invest and start making bigger profits.

By now, you should be up and running!

And so, let me welcome you to the world of excellence! Success and excellence always go hand in hand, and the beauty is that you can achieve excellence in almost everything! The key is to identify and describe what your pursuit will be! What your so-called chosen path will be is not for anyone else to complete it because, when done right, it is all about you, what you love to do, and whatever you know how to do best.

Does it not make sense that if you follow something that you are good at and enjoy, it will make you more successful in the end? Of course, it is! The theme of excellence I'm talking about here has two important points - being good about a field of interest and loving it more dearly. This combination is a great asset in the world of success, especially when it is a path you have set for yourself!

THINK LIKE A MILLIONAIRE

Whatever you like to do, which you find yourself good at, should be at the top of your list of pursuits to excel with much more ease. Next on your list will be things you love to do that you think you can develop as a skill, transforming what can be fun into something worthwhile to excel at. Lastly, we have some things you are good at, but you don't like doing them. These things can become pursuits of excellence but beware of things that may not interest you, no matter how beneficial they may be. There is more to becoming a successful person than just making money.

From me to you.

Resources

Online Publications

Planning Your Retirement Using The Monte Carlo Simulation – Investopedia

All of the World's Stock Exchanges by Size - **Visual Capitalist**

Fundrise Adds Big Name Investors Including Ratner Elghanayan Guggenheim Funding Now 38 Million - **Crowdfund Insider**

Renren-backed Fundrise Bulks-up In Real Estate Crowdfunding Sector - **WSJ**

Investing in Foreclosures For Beginners. **Distressed Real Estate Institute. Archived from** the original

How young investors are chasing early retirement. **Albany Business Review.**

On Efficiently Financing Retirement - **Federal Reserve Bank of Minneapolis**

Emergency Fund - Economic Times – **Indiatimes**

Emergency fund – **Investopedia**

Resources - **LGMA**

Clearing House Definition & Example | Investing Answers - **Investing Answers**

How to make an emergency fund - **Save Invest Retire**

THINK LIKE A MILLIONAIRE

Bitcoin And Crypto Market Smashes Through $2 Trillion As The Price Of Ethereum, Binance Coin, Litecoin And Ripple's XRP Suddenly Soar - **Forbes**

Increase Savings and Rebuild Your Emergency Fund - **Smart About Money**

Wary of Bitcoin? A guide to some other cryptocurrencies - **Ars Technica**

How to Start Investing in Stocks: A Beginner's Guide – Investopedia

7 - My Money Coach

World's 10 Greatest Investors - **Yahoo Finance**

Books

Hershey, Douglas A.; Jacobs-Lawson, Joy M.; McArdle, John J.; Hamagami, Fumiaki (2007). "Psychological Foundations of Financial Planning for Retirement"

Stringham, Edward Peter; Curott, Nicholas A. (2015), 'On the Origins of Stock Markets,'. (Oxford University Press, 2015, pp. 324–344

Notes section

JOSH GRANT

THINK LIKE A MILLIONAIRE

www.ingramcontent.com/pod-product-compliance
Lightning Source LLC
Chambersburg PA
CBHW031414210526
45464CB00005B/1884